The Symphonies of Havergal Brian

Volume One: Symphonies 1–12

To Robert Simpson

Malcolm MacDonald

The Symphonies of Havergal Brian

Volume One: Symphonies 1–12

A CRESCENDO BOOK
TAPLINGER PUBLISHING COMPANY, NEW YORK

Published in 1978 by Taplinger Publishing Company,
New York
Copyright © 1974 Malcolm MacDonald
This book may not be reproduced in whole or in
part without permission. Application with regard to
any use of any part of this volume should be addressed
to the publishers.

The music examples listed below are reproduced by kind
permission of the following publishers:
Symphony No. 1, *The Gothic*: Cranz & Co., London
Symphonies Nos. 2, 8 and 10: Musica Viva, Chelmsford

The text of Lord Alfred Douglas's 'Wine of Summer' is
reproduced with acknowledgements to the publishers, Secker
& Warburg Ltd.

The author wishes to express his gratitude to the composer's
daughter, Mrs. Jean Furnivall, for making available the
sketches of the symphonies; and to record his debt in general
to those whose aid and kindness he hopes to acknowledge
individually at the completion of his second volume.

ISBN 0-8008-7527-3

Printed in England by Tinling (1973) Ltd,
Prescot, Lancs.
(a member of the Oxley Printing Group Ltd)

Contents

1 Introduction: Havergal Brian Symphonist

'Why an Ear, a whirlpool fierce to draw creations in?'
William Blake, *The Book of Thel*

This is a study of the most prolific writer of symphonies since Haydn. One would have liked to have said, the most prolific living symphonist: but sadly, this book was only half written before the announcement of the death of Havergal Brian, on November 28, 1972, two months short of his 97th birthday. With his passing the world lost a powerful, original, but almost unnoticed figure in the music of our time. His death also closed an era, for Brian was the last representative of a great generation of English composers – the generation of Vaughan Williams, Holst, Bax and Ireland, the vanguard of the so-called 'English Musical Renaissance', who built upon the pioneering achievements of Elgar and Delius, consolidated the reputation of English music, and extended it mightily in richness and diversity.

William Havergal Brian was the forgotten member of that generation. Born in Dresden, Staffordshire in 1876, the son of a pottery-worker, he was largely self-taught. Before the Great War his early choral and orchestral works enjoyed a certain vogue, and he was regarded as one of the most talented 'modernists' among younger British composers. But after 1922 performances of his music virtually ceased, and he himself was reduced for a time to the direst poverty. In 1926 he became assistant editor of *Musical Opinion*. Through that journal he waged a lively campaign for all kinds of modern music except his own; and under the editorial pseudonym of 'La Main Gauche' attacked the lack of enterprise of established academicism, concert organizations, and on occasion the B.B.C. He retired in 1940, and in 1958 settled in Sussex, where he continued quietly writing music, as he had done all his life. In 1968, when he was 92, his *oeuvre* included 32 symphonies, no less than 21 of them written since the age of 80.

Such a prodigious flowering of creative energy so late in a composer's career is without parallel, and puts in the shade the illustrious examples of Verdi and Janáček. At the end of his life Brian was no mere relic from a distant past, but a contemporary composer still. Yet for over 30 years none of his post-1919 works was performed, and even the publication in 1945 of Reginald Nettel's biography of Brian, *Ordeal by Music*, had no immediate result. Only in the 1950's, through the enthusiasm of Robert Simpson at the B.B.C., were any of the mature works heard. Such hearings have remained infrequent, the most important being the public performances in 1961 and 1966 of Brian's enormous First Symphony, *The Gothic*.

The interest such performances aroused gained Brian, in his last years, a slight popular notoriety on four counts: his longevity, his extraordinary life of hardship and neglect, the number of his symphonies, and the outsize orchestral demands of one work, *The Gothic*. In turn, these gave rise to the misconceptions that he was an 'amateur' composer, wholly out of touch with the music of his time, naïvely writing one colossal, unperformable work after another. In fact, Brian's command of the orchestra is as 'professional' as one might expect from a man who learned instrumental technique at first hand from the finest virtuoso players of his day; his musical journalism, with its championship of figures as varied as Bartók, Schoenberg, and Varèse, displays a wider, more sympathetic knowledge of developments outside Britain than almost any of his contemporaries possessed; and only two of his works (*The Gothic* and the cantata *Prometheus Unbound*) are of inordinate size. But mistaken impressions have easily gained currency. At the time of his death no music of Brian's had ever been available on record, and no work of importance had been published since 1932. Ninety-five per cent of his huge output, including 4 operas and 50 orchestral works, remained in manuscript, while several other scores have been lost or destroyed. Thus a thorough knowledge of his music has, of necessity, been confined to a tiny number of enthusiasts, with all the suspicions of special pleading that entails. Yet a close study reveals, not a parochial minor figure, but a composer of truly European stature: Brian's achievements as a symphonist, in particular, seem scarcely less impressive than those of Mahler, or Sibelius.

A sceptical reader may well ask why, in that case, Brian's music could be so totally neglected? There is no simple answer, only a melancholy tangle of circumstances. The composer himself was never greatly interested in 'pushing' his own works: between the wars he was too busy trying to earn enough to support his family, and later, as he once remarked, all the people he would have liked to hear his music were dead. Also Brian's name was popularly associated (and perhaps still is) with waning composers like Bantock and Holbrooke, whose pale late-romantic idioms had quickly 'dated', crowded out by the more robust 'Englishness' of Vaughan Williams and Holst, and the rising stars of the Bliss–Walton generation. Consequently few people were aware of what he was actually writing, and most of those little understood it (one reviewer of the piano *Miniatures*, published in 1920, likened them to Schoenberg; another, equally implausibly, to Satie!). The nature of his bigger works militated against performance. They use large orchestras and are quite uncompromising in their demands on instrumental technique. The music rewards close study, but is difficult to play; the highly personal orchestral style creates problems of balance (though no greater than in many other 20th-century composers); and the original formal processes pose taxing problems of structural articulation for the conductor. Thus adequate renderings require numerous and thorough rehearsals; in a word, it is *expensive* music to produce. To all these naturally inconvenient factors it must be added that in loss of scores, death of sponsors, mismanagement by publishers, commercial naïvety, and sheer ill-luck, Brian proved accident-prone to a degree.

A final point: it is a myth that music of high quality finds its audience unaided. Of course quality of inspiration is the ultimate criterion for survival, but it is precisely the ultimate values which take longest to establish. Elgar, Tovey and Richard Strauss thought Brian a great composer: but though a reputation may be deserved, it has to be *made,* and in the last resort it is made by publicity; often – whether we like it or not – simply by fashion. Havergal Brian was well aware of this. He once wrote of the obituaries that followed Elgar's death:

> What I don't like . . . is the comforting suggestion to the English people that they did not neglect Elgar . . . I say very positively that in the early years Elgar's music had to be stuffed into the ears of the British public by a body of friends such as composers of his quality have rarely had.

Brian knew what he was talking about, for he was one of those friends. He had such friends too, but they were fewer, and their opportunities for informed advocacy much less.

So this book attempts to draw attention to a body of work that is still almost totally unknown. Brian made striking contributions to all the major genres except chamber music: his operas, for example, deserve a book to themselves. But the 32 symphonies form the core of his output. It was here, perhaps, that he achieved most, and so here any close scrutiny of his *oeuvre* must begin.

The completed survey will comprise 2 volumes. The present one sketches Brian's musical development as far as the writing of *The Gothic*; then proceeds to examine, chapter by chapter, each of the first 12 symphonies, composed between 1919 and 1957. The approach is primarily (but by no means exclusively) descriptive, for, at present, general knowledge of Brian's music is hardly such as to render description superfluous. Volume II, which will follow as soon as possible, will deal similarly with the remaining 20 symphonies – the incredible harvest of the years 1959–68 – and will contain further chapters on such general topics as Brian's methods of work, his orchestration, and his approach to symphonic structure. In a final chapter, I shall attempt an assessment of the significance of the symphonies and the creative achievement they represent. My hope is that the reader will find grounds for such an assessment emerging naturally as the book proceeds.

However, some preliminary remarks are in order, to indicate where Brian stands in 20th-century music. I trust I may be forgiven for setting aside the fashionable view that 'the Symphony is dead' – that it is no longer a 'meaningful' form. In the past 200 years, 'Symphony' has come to mean more than a set of structural principles; essentially it implies the highest, most sophisticated kind of musical thought, combining and employing organically all music's constituent elements, attaining thereby something of the profundity of philosophy and the sublimity of poetry, and expressed through the most challenging of all instrumental mediums – the modern orchestra. As such, it is one of the central facts of Western civilization; if it is dead, so are all of us. But the work of such very different contemporary composers as Shostakovich, Roberto Gerhard, Lutoslawski, Roger Sessions, Robert Simpson, Benjamin Frankel and Havergal Brian allays any fears for its health; and amongst these Havergal Brian's achievement, because the largest and hardest-won, is perhaps the most encouraging of all.

It should be realised that Brian was the first English composer of stature – perhaps in truth the first English composer – from the industrial working classes. This fact was never a handicap with professional musicians, who always accepted him as an equal, but it certainly conditioned the peculiar difficulties of his struggle for recognition, and his inability to carve out a proper career. It also profoundly shaped his musical character in a host of ways. He was essentially a self-made composer, and in that he resembles Elgar; but he began even further down the social scale, with correspondingly greater disadvantages.

Elgar was Brian's first model, and though he early outgrew his direct influence, he was heir to certain aspects of Elgar's style – especially his flamboyant orchestral polyphony and adventurous brass writing. Doubtless Brian would have been amply content to be regarded as in some sense Elgar's successor, but his music has also a European dimension even stronger than Elgar's. If Elgar, Brian, and in their lesser way Bantock and Holbrooke stood for anything, it was for the creation of an English music without self-conscious 'Englishness' or slavish imitation of German models, which would beat the Austro-German musical tradition on its own ground and with its own weapons. Brian, whose music is in many ways profoundly English, went furthest towards that ideal. Although largely self-educated (he left school at the age of 12) he very early gained a wide knowledge of German language and literature which greatly extended his imaginative horizons. He had an abiding (though by no means uncritical) admiration of German culture; and his lifelong artistic dialogue with it, from his first setting of Goethe in 1896 to his 4-act opera *Faust*, 60 years later, is evidence that Britain was, in a sense, too small a milieu for him. Brian's symphonies must therefore be judged outside their merely British context, by reference to the greatest European symphonists of the century.

I earlier mentioned Mahler and Sibelius, because these two composers stand as the opposite poles of 20th-century symphonic thought: the arch-Romantic, for whom a symphony must express the whole world, and the Classic, for whom it must create a profound inner logic by stylistic unity and severity of form. Havergal

Brian's symphonies occupy a position almost exactly between these antipodes, and suggest that their opposition may be more apparent than real. Like Mahler, Brian draws upon 'popular' styles (especially the spirit of the march) for expressive imagery: the great pre-1900 brass bands echo in sublimated form through much of his mature music. The structural implications of these 'popular' elements, as in Mahler, are far from primitive. With Sibelius, on the other hand, Brian shares a concern to enlarge structural resources by accomodating extremes of motion, from 'Wagnerian' slowness to 'classical' allegro activity, within the limits of a single form. Whereas Sibelius *reconciled* these extremes by imperceptible transitions from one to the other, Brian brings them into direct *confrontation*, yoking them by violence together, often dispensing with transitions entirely. The result is a rough-hewn music of great inner tension, in which dramatic opposition of extremes extends not only to movement but to texture, harmony, melodic style and expressive character. But the contrasting elements are made to throw light on one another: they exist not for themselves, but as the (sometimes momentary) embodiments of a dynamic process of sustained thought, helping to create the overall momentum and character of each work.

Such music is not easy to grasp at first hearing. Complex, idiosyncratic, at times almost abrasive, it can repel facile sympathy. It has to be struggled with before its logic and rightness become apparent. Yet it exerts an irresistible fascination and the rewards for perseverance are immense. I hope to communicate something of its fascinating atmosphere, so unlike that of any other music of our time. Whether or not Brian's symphonies 'express the whole world', they certainly seem to *create* their own world; and when the imagery of the music suggests, as it so often does, fantastic landscapes and rumours of war, we are justified in relating its world to that of epic. It would not be inappropriate to regard the symphonies as one mighty epic whose 32 books, with their obsessive march-rhythms and sense of ceaseless exploration, contain something of both Iliad and Odyssey.

But it is an epic of our own century. All music is inescapably an expression of time and place, be it a workers' song or a string quartet, and exists both for its own time and for posterity. Brian's earlier works have already been denied that first stage of existence, and it is fruitless, though fascinating, to speculate what effect works as unique as the *Gothic* Symphony and the opera *The Tigers* might have had in performance at the time of their completion. They still belong to history, but their chance to influence contemporaries has long passed. Yet the majority of Brian's symphonies (27 of them, in fact) were written after 1945. They are contemporary works still, by a composer who never ceased to look forward: a composer who, born in the year of the first production of *The Ring* at Bayreuth, lived to take an interest in the first production of Peter Maxwell Davies's *Taverner*. There is much to be learned here, not least about the doggedness of the human spirit. The music speaks to us with the voice of a man who survived a terrible century, ignored but undefeated, striving to work out his own musical salvation. There is, perhaps, little comfort in his music, but much courage; and the courage can be an inspiration.

Havergal Brian died with his life-work complete; but even in his last few years, when he wrote nothing new, he still took a lively interest in the *future* of music, of which he was more optimistic than many. If it sometimes seems there is *no* future – that, in pulling in so many directions at once, contemporary music has lost all direction, isolating the major creators and causing the lesser, in despair, to seek refuge in passing fashion – it may be because we have made little attempt to understand the recent past. The road forward must be lit by a reassessment of the great figures who first pointed out that road, and helped to build it: be they honoured but little-understood, like Schoenberg and Debussy; or vaguely-respected and even less understood, like Busoni; or such as Havergal Brian, who in his lifetime was hardly even noticed, and for whom an assessment, however partial, is long overdue. If an account of his symphonies even slightly alters our conception of music in the 20th century, this study will have served some purpose.

2   The Path to the Symphony
     (1896–1919)

'If a man does not keep pace with his companions, perhaps it is because he hears a different drummer. Let him march to the music which he hears, however measured or far away.'   Thoreau

Havergal Brian had been writing music for over a quarter of a century before his first true symphony, the legendary *Gothic,* was begun. It is thus no early work, but the creation of a fully-mature musical mind. The inner workings of that mind, like the creative urge that impelled the composer to produce mighty work after mighty work, will always remain mysterious. But we can at least point to some of the things that affected its development in the years before *The Gothic* was begun.

The opportunities for an academic musical education were slim, to say the least, for the son of an ordinary worker in the Staffordshire Potteries in the late 19th century. Apart from a thorough grounding in harmony and counterpoint from a local music-teacher at the age of 14, Brian was an entirely self-taught composer. It was probably a blessing in disguise. A college or university training (Brian's father quashed his chances of an organ scholarship to St. John's, Cambridge) could only have conventionalized him. Left to his own devices, he was able to develop his individuality to a striking degree. In a rare autobiographical reminiscence[1], he once recalled that his earliest musical memories were of being fascinated by the vibrations set up by the deepest pedal of a church organ; being so captivated by the beat of the big drum in a village band that he played truant from school to follow it for miles; and hearing 3 crack brass bands in competition, playing selections from *The Damnation of Faust.* These impressions of a very young boy are significant in view of the character of Brian's own music, with its deep basses, march-rhythms, heavy percussion, and magisterial brass writing. It does

[1] 'The Faraway Years', *Musical Opinion,* January 1949, p. 179.

not seem implausible to suggest that Brian's avoidance of academic training enabled him to preserve something of his child-hood wonder and delight in such sounds, and helped to lay the foundations of his own personal style.

His self-education was thenceforth in the honourable school of practical and amateur music-making. Originally a treble soloist in a church choir, he learned the organ and by the age of 14 had become a church organist with the salary of £12 a year. He also learned the violin, but (like Schoenberg) abandoned it for the cello, on which he played Haydn, Mozart, and early Beethoven in an amateur string quartet. Later he played piano and cello in vaudeville bands and theatre orchestras. And all the time he was hearing more and more music, for he grew up in the era of the great North Staffordshire Triennial Festivals, when the 'Five Towns' were an important centre of English musical life. He discovered the music of Grieg, heard the Carl Rosa company in *The Flying Dutchman, Meistersinger,* and *Pagliacci,* and was intro-duced to the music of Schumann and Brahms by the great local conductor Swinnerton Heap. He heard Beethoven's Ninth for the first time in Hanley in 1896, and the next year regularly attended the Hallé concerts in Manchester under Hans Richter. Later still he sat in upon the rehearsals of J. G. Halford's orchestra in Birmingham, and pored over the scores in their library. It was a haphazard road to personal mastery, perhaps, but a royal one.

Brian appears to have begun composing at a very early age: by the time he was 12, having been apprenticed to a joiner, he was covering white deal boards with organ music, marches and waltzes – and thereby losing his job. But it was not until 1896, when the first performance of Elgar's *King Olaf* came to him as a blinding revelation of what a virtually self-taught British musician could do, that Brian decided to devote his life to composition. It was a brave, almost suicidal, decision. Elgar himself had hardly 'arrived', though he had been struggling for recognition for over a decade. Without patronage or an academic post, the English composer of serious music could hardly expect to make a living, far less experience popular success. What chance had Brian, lack-ing the first, unsuited for the second? Considering the uncom-promising nature of his music, it is surprising that he did manage, before the Great War, to establish a modest reputation.

His earliest, pre-1900 works are lost. They included a *Requiem* and a *Tragic Prelude* for orchestra. His first surviving orchestral piece is a concert overture, *For Valour* (1902), inspired by Walt Whitman's 'Drum Taps'. It is a remarkable work in several respects, above all in its complete freedom from outside influences. Though the stylistic ambience is late-Romantic, in the manner of Elgar, Strauss and Tchaikovsky, one can point to no specific echo of these composers, and the music has a rugged strength that, to a student of his later works, already bespeaks Havergal Brian and no other composer. *For Valour* is laid out as an extended sonata-form in C and E (the coexistence of these two keys is a recurrent, almost obsessive, feature of Brian's earlier works). However, Brian modifies the conventional design, creating a much more 'open' form: the recapitulation ushers in, not a coda, but a new exposition that ends the overture with a triumphant statement of entirely fresh material – doubtless following Whitman's line 'To fiercer, weightier battles give expression'. The handling of the large-scale form is as original as it is assured, and must have suggested to sympathetic ears that if the composer of *For Valour* were to turn his attention to a full-scale symphony, he might achieve some splendid results.

That time was still far off. There are two distinct strains in Brian's early music: one weighty, martial and heroic, as embodied in *For Valour*; the other a satirical, snook-cocking irreverence. The latter quality now came to the fore in his orchestral music, while his more serious side went into a series of large choral works – *Psalm XXIII* (1901), *By the Waters of Babylon* (1903), and *The Vision of Cleopatra* (1907–8). It was inevitable that a composer brought up in the great choral traditions of the Potteries should write cantatas – however strange they might seem to local critics – but his preference was clearly for orchestral wizardry. A work like the *English Suite No. 1* (1899–1904), with its rowdy 'fairground' finale like an English *Petrushka* (anticipating Stravinsky's work by a decade), hardly seems the work of the same composer as *By the Waters,* whose noble orchestral prelude has a loftiness of expression that is post-*Gerontius* in spirit. It is almost as if Brian were thumbing his nose at his own predilection for seriousness. And indeed, though he could produce deeply-felt, passionate music, he must have felt suspicious of the conventional moulds into which custom forced him to pour it; must have sensed,

stirring within him, the capacity to do something wholly individual, quite different from Strauss, Elgar, Delius and Bantock.
At least the satirical vein, in which he anticipated the spirit of the
lighter Bliss, Walton and Lambert, was distinctively his own,
and so he gave it full rein.

Yet in 1906, apparently, Brian was seriously considering a full-
scale, 4-movement Symphony – the first seed of *The Gothic*. But
Ernest Newman, to whom he broached the idea, was dis-
couraging: the conventional symphony had had its day, he
thought. So when, the following year, Brian completed a work
entitled *A Fantastic Symphony*, it proved to be another piece of
musical humour: a 3-movement commentary on the tale of the
Three Blind Mice. The first movement was a flamboyant set of
variations on the nursery-rhyme tune, the second a scherzo de-
picting the souls of the mice flitting to paradise, and the finale
was headed 'Dance of the Farmer's Wife'. However, the scherzo
was subsequently lost and the outer movements were published
separately as *Fantastic Variations on an Old Rhyme* and *Festal Dance*:
although they were held to constitute a 'Symphony No. 1' until
as recently as 1967, when Brian finally revised the numbering of
his symphonies. In fact they are quite independent pieces, sharing
only the same key – E major – and scored for very different forces.
The *Variations* include an organ, while *Festal Dance* – a remarkable
tour-de-force which is the ancestor of several of Brian's later
scherzo-movements – opens with a passage for unaccompanied
percussion, and features a furiously virtuosic piano part, fancifully
described in the score as being *ad. lib*. Although both pieces are
well worth revival, they suggest that Brian's first symphonic
attempt had no pretensions to profundity.

The year of the *Fantastic Symphony* also saw Brian's rise to
modest fame. Henry Wood gave both *For Valour* and the *English
Suite* during the 1907 Proms, with great success. Going down to
Queen's Hall in his carriage on the night of the latter performance,
Wood suggested to Brian the idea of another suite: one that, in
addition to the normal orchestra, would feature all the older
instruments that had fallen out of use – the oboe d'amore, bass
oboe, bassett-horn, pedal clarinet and so on. Brian was intrigued –
but when he discussed the scheme with his great friend Granville
Bantock, the older composer dissuaded him on the reasonable
grounds that such a work would need a great deal of preparation

in return for very few performances. Nevertheless, the idea had taken root in Brian's mind.

The following year, Thomas Beecham premièred (and then lost without trace) Brian's symphonic poem *Hero and Leander* in Hanley. Bantock performed *For Valour* in Liverpool, and at this concert Brian sat next to Delius, whose *Brigg Fair* was being given its first English performance. In 1909, Brian's work was featured during the first festival of the ill-fated Musical League, and his most ambitious pre-War work, the big cantata *The Vision of Cleopatra*, received its first (and only) performance at the Southport Festival. Brian had even found a patron, and was temporarily free from money problems: his future seemed almost bright. Yet in fact he had already reached the apogee of his fame.

His range of expression was widening and deepening. When, after a period of song-writing, he returned to orchestral composition in 1911, the two works he produced were in many respects his most 'symphonic' conceptions so far. Moreover, the Comedy Overture *Doctor Merryheart* and the Tone Poem *In Memoriam*, a highly-contrasting pair, seem to present the expressive dichotomy of Brian's early style in radical form. *Merryheart*, with its gorgeous orchestration and bizarrely-detailed programme, is both a homage to and an affectionate send-up of the Straussian heroic tone poem, with parodic side-swipes at Elgar's *nobilmente* vein and Wagnerian dragons. Like Strauss's *Don Quixote*, it is cast as a set of symphonic variations, whose scheme is ingeniously accommodated to sonata form. *In Memoriam,* by contrast, is a grand symphonic funeral march – perhaps Brian's first fully-mature work, and one of the earliest of the sublimations of the funeral-march spirit that were to play such a crucial role in his music.

Doctor Merryheart was premièred at the second and last of the Musical League's festivals, in Birmingham in January 1913; and Henry Wood introduced it at the Proms in the same year. Most of Brian's works had begun to get into print, but already the composer was in difficulties. After quarrelling with his patron, and thus losing financial security, he had moved to London in search of work, publishers, and performances, with almost complete lack of success. He produced a wealth of songs and part-songs as pot-boilers, but no firm was really interested, and he was soon living in real poverty.

Then the Great War broke out: the War which, among it

many effects, was to sweep away the musical world with which Brian had been associated. Performance of his music virtually ceased. The war had a profound effect on the composer himself. At its outbreak he patriotically enlisted in Kitchener's Army and, though he never saw service at the front, became sadly familiar with the disillusionment and petty brutality of life in camp. Invalided out with a hand injury, he next secured a job examining and listing the effects of men killed serving with the Canadian forces – and this gave him a graphic insight into the useless barbarism that was taking place in the trenches.

The experience left its mark; and when, in 1916, Brian resigned his job and went to work in Birmingham, he began almost at once to sketch an enormous comic opera, both a reaction and an artistic revenge – an almost surreal satire on military life and war-time England, from the standpoint of the ordinary soldier. *The Tigers* is his first masterpiece, and possibly the most original of all his works. Brian's libretto preaches no sermons and passes no judgements, but presents a goon-like picture of a society that is chaotic, superficial, and utterly insincere – while the music, for the most part wildly funny, hints now and then at undercurrents of the blackest tragedy. It is a dream-vision separated from night-mare by the thinnest of lines: its message, insofar as it has one, is that men cannot stand too much reality – against War, laughter is the only defence.

Stylistically *The Tigers* capitalises, in an astonishingly rich and varied way, on the vein of parody and burlesque in Brian's earlier music – allied to a brilliant, hitherto unsuspected command of stage-craft and theatrical effect. There is a recurrent 'Music-hall' flavour; the 'fairground' images of the First *English Suite* now come to life on the stage (the opera opens in the midst of a Bank Holiday carnival on Hampstead Heath); and the spirit of *Festal Dance* gives birth to wilder and more sinister offspring in two of the work's five 'Symphonic Dances', *Wild Horsemen* and *Gargoyles*. In the view of the present writer, *The Tigers* – never yet staged – may prove to be the greatest English comic opera. Its composi-tion, an incredible feat of creative imagination for its time and place, announced Brian's arrival at full artistic maturity. It also put a grand and final seal on his first period of development.

By the time *The Tigers* was complete in vocal score, the War was almost over. Ironically, had it been possible to stage the opera in the immediate post-War years, it would almost certainly have gained acceptance and earned its composer acclaim, for it would have accorded with the new, cynical spirit of the 1920's. But a production was far beyond Brian's means. Moreover, he was turning in another direction. His satirical works of the pre-war period had certainly anticipated the music of the new generation in some respects, and in *The Tigers* had yielded an enormous expressive harvest. But beyond *The Tigers* what more could be done in that vein? And was flippancy and grotesque, after all, a valid response in a world that had been torn so grievously apart by global war? Brian, now in his forties, thought not; and so, as musical satire became chic and popular, he renounced it and – one may surmise – looked inward, in an attempt to understand, rather than caricature, human experience. Now his music assumed the searching, exploratory qualities that were to persist throughout his later works.

The immediate result was a number of songs whose darkly emotional tone places them among the most bitterly subjective music Brian ever wrote. Especially the almost histrionic *The Soul of Steel* and *The Defiled Sanctuary*, where the impassioned setting of William Blake's final lines

> *So I turn'd into a sty*
> *And laid me down among the swine*

suggests that an anguish of soul is not merely being depicted but experienced.

From this grim new beginning, Brian's music gropes towards a kind of objectivity. The next major work he planned also took its subject from Blake: a cantata based on that parable of the bitterness of mortality, *The Book of Thel*. But the piece never reached completion: it seems likely that Brian's imagination had already been fired by the looming outlines of a conception incomparably vaster. A Third *English Suite,* not so much humorous as experimental in tone, was completed in mid-1919, and soon afterwards Brian began writing a true symphony at last.

Many influences from earlier years were coming together to produce his most sustained creative effort yet. The 1906 idea for a serious symphony had become entwined with Henry Wood's suggestion about the obsolete instruments – not for novelty value, but because they would provide an orchestra complete in

every department, and make available an unprecedented variety
of timbre. The initial spur for composition came from Goethe's
Faust: Goethe, whom Brian had been reading for years and who
had been one of his most powerful literary influences. But from
the timeless figure of Faust Brian was drawn on, to a vision of
the mediaeval period in which Faust was supposed to have lived,
and which had fired Goethe's imagination. Especially to the
architecture of that time, the huge Gothic cathedrals with their
vaulted spaces and disposition of light – as a boy, Brian had been
overwhelmed by their grandeur, typified in the Staffordshire area
by Lichfield Cathedral. His original plan was to set a section of
Faust, Part II for his symphony's finale (not knowing that Mahler
had done the same in his Eighth); but, in Brian's own words,
another text 'pushed itself forward as the only possible finale'.
The work was to conclude with a choral setting of the *Te Deum*
on an unparalleled scale, for solo voices, choruses, orchestra, and
brass bands. The whole conception added up to a mighty *Gothic*
Symphony, a great cathedral in sound.

The work was sketched between 1919 and 1922, though unlike
most of the other symphonies we do not know the exact dates. It
was a vast venture into the unknown, and Brian felt his way
forward with care, writing several smaller works as contrapuntal
studies for the mighty fabric of the finale. These include three
fugal pieces for piano, the largest of which – the monumental
Double Fugue in E flat – presages the musical language of his
later years. The Fourth *English Suite* of 1921 – probably written
between the first and second parts of the symphony – also looks
like a study, this time in instrumental sonorities.

But *The Gothic* accorded neither with the spirit nor the eco-
nomic realities of the time. Brian hardly expected it would ever
be performed. Yet its composition seems to have been a psychological necessity. Against the brutal and destructive aspects of
human life, he may subconsciously have been pitting his personal
creative powers – raising, bar by bar, this immense musical edifice
as answer and antithesis to the forces of inhumanity that the Great
War had unleashed. The printed score bears a significant quotation
from *Faust*. Translated, it runs

> *Whoever strives with all his might,*
> *That man we can redeem.*

Writing the symphony sustained Brian through a period of great personal hardship. He had begun the work while living in Lewes. Later he continued it at Moulscoombe, near Brighton, where the invigorating scenery of the South Downs was another spur to composition. To support his wife and family he was forced to rely entirely upon musical hack-work, copying scores at 6d. a page and drawing up orchestral parts. The task was not without occasional interest (he was employed, for instance, on the percussion parts of Varèse's *Amériques*), but it was impossible to make more than a bare subsistence in those conditions. Brian, short of food and under mental strain, worked on the full score of *The Gothic* late in the nights; when no hack-work was forthcoming, it was his only pursuit. How much it meant to him may be guessed from the fact that the autograph score is the most exquisitely, painstakingly calligraphed of all his manuscripts.

He had little encouragement. Henry Wood saw the completed score of the first part of the symphony and the sketches of the second, but though he admired the work thought the cost of rehearsals would be prohibitive. Eugene Goossens intended to introduce some extracts from *The Tigers* at a series of concerts, but the plan collapsed on the death of his sponsor. Even when Brian secured the post of deputy editor of *Musical Opinion* and moved to London, there were no performances of his music. Still he toiled on with *The Gothic*. At the suggestion of Sir Hugh Allen, he pasted together sheets of 26- and 28-stave music paper to form the vast 54-stave pages he needed for Part II. These were bound into a single volume, and in 1927, on its very last page, Havergal Brian completed the full score of the *Gothic* Symphony, after a labour of eight years. Perhaps not even he realised that this was only a beginning.

A NOTE ON THE NUMBERING OF THE SYMPHONIES. As mentioned above, the *Fantastic Symphony,* though no longer extant as such, was long regarded as Symphony No. 1, and the five following symphonies (from *The Gothic* to *Wine of Summer*) as Nos. 2 to 6 inclusive. The *Sinfonia Tragica,* on the other hand, bore no number. In 1967 Brian corrected the anomaly, dropping the *Fantastic Symphony* from the canon, making *The Gothic* to *Wine of Summer* Symphonies 1 to 5, and inserting the *Tragica* in its chronological position as Symphony No. 6. Due to a misunderstanding at the BBC, where the scores were held, the *Tragica* was for a short time regarded as No. 7 and the real Seventh was broadcast as No. 6. The mistake has since been rectified. I have employed the 1967 numbering, with *The Gothic* as No. 1 and the *Tragica* as No. 6, throughout this book.

3 'The Gothic': Symphony No. 1 in D minor (1919–27)

Brian's *Gothic* Symphony is the crucial work of his entire career; a voyage of exploration in uncharted regions; and his own discovery of himself as a symphonist on the epic scale. In the previous chapter, I sketched some of the elements which inspired it. But above all, 'Gothic' meant to Brian an age of almost unlimited expansion of human knowledge, both secular and spiritual. His symphony recreates that in 20th-century terms. It is a work profoundly involved with tradition, which is 'about' reaching out into the unknown, a Leap in the Dark. It has its miscalculations, but ultimately its strengths far outweigh any weaknesses: it speaks with the unmistakable voice of greatness. On those who know the score, it exerts a tremendous fascination, and it is utterly unique – a book could be devoted to it alone.[1]

Nearly 40 chequered years elapsed between the symphony's completion and its first performance. In 1928 Brian entered it in the Columbia Graphophone Company's Schubert Centenary Competition, for a completion of Schubert's *Unfinished* Symphony or a new orchestral work: it gained second prize in the British division, and Brian was awarded £50. The score then went to Vienna for the judgement of the world prize. There the international jury (which included Tovey, Nielsen, and Glazunov) awarded the £2,000 prize to Kurt Atterberg, though Brian believed they had deliberated all day before choosing, by Glazunov's casting vote, between Atterberg and himself. Brian got nothing.

[1] In fact the most detailed examination of any aspect of Brian's art to date is a 200-page thesis, *Havergal Brian and his Symphony 'The Gothic'*, by Paul Rapoport (University of Illinois, Urbana-Champaign, 1972) – a fascinating study, to which this chapter is indebted for some particulars.

'The Gothic': a page from the manuscript
(Part I, third movement)

Once he had retrieved his score there was talk of performances. Hamilton Harty hoped to mount the work in Manchester, but the depletion of the Hallé's ranks as players departed into the newly-formed B.B.C. orchestra made the scheme impossible. Eugene Goossens, who considered *The Gothic* 'an outstanding master-piece', laboured mightily to present it at the 1935 Cincinnati Biennial Festival – but the effect of the Depression era had reduced the Festival's resources to a point where they were inadequate to cover the many rehearsals and vast orchestral and choral forces required, so that the idea was abandoned in 1934.

Meanwhile, the huge score had actually found its way into print. A director of the continental publishers Cranz & Co. saw Brian's works in manuscript, was immediately impressed, and decided to undertake publication. Richard Strauss, to whom Brian dedicated *The Gothic*, may also have used his influence here. In 1932, Cranz issued a handsome vocal score of *The Tigers*, and an enormous 2-volume full score of *The Gothic*. This seems a rare act of philanthropy! The cost of engraving was immense, and 40 years later Cranz are nowhere near recouping the money invested in Brian's music. For the mere existence of a published score (which, sadly, is a mare's nest of printing errors) brought per-formance no nearer. *The Gothic* remained a mythical giant, for-gotten during the war years (when Cranz, as an 'alien' firm, remained inactive). Not until Dr. Robert Simpson became interested in Brian in the early 1950's did anyone have the vision actively to promote it. At last, on June 24, 1961, the huge work was premièred by partly amateur forces under the baton of Bryan Fairfax in Westminster Hall; and 5 years later came the first fully professional performance, at the Albert Hall on October 30, 1966, conducted by Sir Adrian Boult.[1] The auditorium was packed, and at the end Havergal Brian, by then 90 years old, received a prolonged standing ovation.

Audience reaction to these performances was on the whole enthusiastic, though not unnaturally tempered with bewilder-ment. Presumably concert-goers lately made familiar with the symphonies of Mahler expected something similar, and were disturbed to be confronted with music of a wholly different kind. Furthermore, the work is so vast as to be almost beyond under-

---

[1] Complete lists of the artists involved in performances will be found in Appen-dix III.

standing on a single hearing. For this reason we need not concern ourselves with the reactions of music critics, except to note that they were very mixed.

The Gothic has been represented as a 4-movement symphony with an excessively long choral finale. Actually it is a symphony in six movements, divided into an orchestral Part I and a choral-and-orchestral Part II of 3 movements each, lasting about 31 and 61 minutes respectively. Part I – a symphony in itself – is a transitional work, which moves away from an initially familiar late-Romantic language with ever-increasing stylistic and structural freedom, arriving in the third movement at a fully 20th-century idiom and a completely personal handling of symphonic form. (It is permissible to perform this part on its own.) In contrast, Part II is the longest and most elaborate setting in existence of the *Te Deum* – visionary music, representing a continuation and fulfilment of much that is implicit in Part I.

The orchestra required for Part I is by no means excessive: the normal large symphony orchestra with a fairly large percussion section, supplemented by an organ, a second set of timpani, alto flute[1], oboe d'amore, bass oboe, bassett-horn and cornets.

PART I

1. *Allegro assai*   2. *Lento espressivo e solenne*   3. *Vivace*

The first movement is the least successful part of the symphony – but even so it is a fascinating and exciting piece, among the most powerful music Brian had so far written. It is cast in sonata form, and if the material Brian pours into it threatens to break the mould, that weakness is itself highly revealing.

The very opening commands attention with a superb orchestral gesture, announcing a symphonic thinker of real character:

---

[1] Brian calls this a bass flute, but the alto instrument in G is clearly intended. The oboe d'amore and basset-horn had been used by Strauss, and the bass oboe by Delius.

Two timpanists thunderously echo the stamping figure *x*, confirming D minor, and the first subject leaps into life with a tough, wiry main theme:

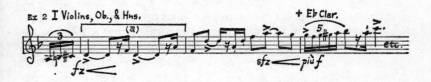

Here the oscillating third of figure *x* extends into a rising triad (figure *2a*) which is to be a unifying element throughout Part I. The music surges on, through a subsidiary canonic figure and a snatch of suaver melody for oboes and violins, to a variation of *2a* loudly proclaimed by trumpets and horns; fierce semiquaver string figuration over a further variant in tubas and trombones; and a quick sequential build-up to a climax, ending in a shimmering chord of B flat minor.

This first-subject exposition (or rather explosion) is highly concentrated: less than 30 bars, less than 45 seconds duration. It gains thereby an effect of impetuous energy and muscular strength to which words do scant justice. But now what happens? The shimmering chord dissolves in a single harp arpeggio; the key changes to D flat major, most languorous of tonalities; and in a sensuous texture of gently-rocking chords on celesta, harps, and divided tremolo *sul ponticello* strings, a solo violin states the principal second subject melody:

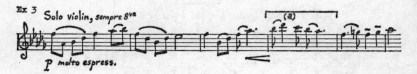

Ex 3

It is a beautiful tune – almost too beautiful. Surely the textbook clichés about 'masculine' first and 'feminine' second subjects were seldom exemplified in such an extreme form. And herein lies the movement's weakness: its two principal themes cancel each other out. Already the boundless momentum of the symphony's opening has vanished as if it had never been, and the music seems to float becalmed.

The hindsight of the later symphonies makes this significant. Extreme contrasts of mood and movement are the life and soul of Brian's style. Even here the abruptness and unexpectedness of the change are wholly characteristic. Clearly, from the first Brian was striving instinctively towards a radically new kind of symphonism: one which demanded more 'open' forms, dramatic opposition rather than integration of extremes, and the generation of an overall momentum through the interplay of many different degrees of movement. Here, however, he has yet to solve the structural problems involved: and the answer does *not* lie in the dynamism and underlying symmetries of conventional sonata form. Exx. 2 and 3 refuse to establish any satisfactory relationship. While one holds sway, the other simply does not exist for us, so that the music, veering between hectic activity and near-immobility, puts almost more strain on the structure than it can bear.

So completely has Ex. 3 taken over that it seems free to expand at its own leisurely pace. First comes a dreamy, descending roulade for 3 flutes in close harmony; then the key shifts to D major for a rather Baxian variation of Ex. 3 on oboe d'amore. This in turn becomes a counterpoint to a long-breathed viola melody whose lyrical line soon passes to the violins. As if striving to regain lost energy, the music modulates to G minor and is briefly stirred by the beating of two timpani. But the problem is not one of keys but of themes. The violins recall figure 3*a*, the tonality brightens towards the major, and though the orchestration grows fuller, there is no real climax: a canonic exchange of 3*a* in the brass leads to *Poco largamente* and a complete restatement of Ex. 3, in D, on oboes and clarinets.

It is all lovely music, but the second-subject exposition has now unfolded to dangerous lengths. The initial momentum must be regained, and quickly. It cannot grow organically out of this music, so Brian, by a simple dramatic stroke, separates off the second subject and begins afresh. Horns and trumpets strike in with a reminiscence of *2a*, flowering into a grand cadence for full brass alone, carrying the music back to D minor.

Tough, eventful, and economical, the development now begins *Allegro assai* with chromatic wailings from the flutes over figure *x* on sinisterly marching bassoons. Then Ex. 2 and the other first-subject elements are pressed into vigorous service by the full orchestra. The old impetus seems firmly regained: but after a canonic passage for 6 horns the music suddenly slows, with soft woodwind tones and a descending harp arpeggio. Over a pedal F, Ex. 3 is heard on solo oboe; and even though Brian combines it with echoes of figure *y* on muted horns, the sudden 'application of the brakes' is dismaying. Luckily he does not pursue Ex. 3 further, but whips up the excitement again by plunging into C sharp minor in 12/8 time, with variants of Ex. 2 in trumpets and horns and a broad, striding tune in the strings. This time the pace really is untrammelled – the music, darker and more powerful than anything heard so far, surges forward in a flood of splendid invention. The mood grows wilder, the writing ever more virtuosic, with bellowing tubas charging up the scale. Figure *2a* is pulled into jagged, angular shapes, and the passage culminates in a great *tutti* outburst, with rising sequences of triplet semi-quavers that seem to set the music spinning like a top.

With a brusqueness that we shall come to know as wholly typical, Brian breaks off this climax at the peak of the excitement to reveal a different vista – of drums beating softly and myster-iously in F Minor. At this wholly unexpected juncture, he brings the development to a close – with a new theme (Ex. 4).[1]

---

[1] Paul Rapoport (*op. cit.*) has convincingly demonstrated that Ex. 4 is cunningly derived from the harmonic premises of the last 2 bars of the first-subject group; however, its effect is of something quite fresh.

The music seems to come to a complete standstill. A cor anglais meditates in melancholy tones, then all is silent. In the stillness, the solo violin enters, unaccompanied, with a slow cadenza-like recitative. It climbs higher and higher in register, and then, in an even lusher texture than before, sings out Ex. 3, lyrical and radiantly sweet, in E major – the first appearance of a key which is to become increasingly important. Brian has begun the recapitulation with the subjects in the reverse order. But he cannot afford to let the second subject over-expand itself a second time, in a movement that has already contained too much slow music for comfort. Instead, he reintroduces Ex. 4, which had so unexpectedly ended the development, in F minor, over echoes of 2a in the timpani – and this more restrained melody does duty for the rest of the second subject group.

Soon a drum-roll on D leads back to D minor and the re-entry of the first subject, *Allegro molto vivace* – which also forms an elaborate coda. Development continues up to the end. Over the stamping figure *x*, trumpets transform the rising triad of 2a into a D–E–G chord progression, pinned back to D minor by figure *y*. But as tension mounts and the music steers into a magnificent climax, the trumpets vary this shape and force the music into E minor, with *y* punctuated by cymbal-smashes. Horns proclaim 2a in full-throated augmentation and the music appears to be racing to a conclusion – but then the brakes are applied with a vengeance. There is a sudden rallentando, and Ex. 3 sounds from afar, in a foreign B major, on flutes, oboes and bassett-horn. Violins and violas take it up, and with 3a very prominent the music swells towards a climax; but now it seems too slow to achieve a decisive end, for Ex. 3 cannot generate sufficient pace. Brian saves matters by a final dramatic stroke: there is a blast of tone from full organ (not heard until this moment), and the movement ends in a thunder of drums on *x*, and an abrupt, weighty triad of D major.

Despite its awkwardnesses this is a powerful, original movement which infinitely repays study. The introduction of Ex. 4 and its use in the recapitulation are effective modifications of sonata-design. The key-scheme is unorthodox: D flat major (second subject), becoming C sharp minor (development), prepares the prominent E major–minor of the recapitulation, obliquely re-called by the B major interruption in the coda. These moves towards E are quite foreign to the tonic D minor – but E major is the goal of the whole symphony.

One of the most striking features of Part I of *The Gothic* is the growing sense of mastery that informs it. The first movement is powerful, but form and content are at odds. The second move-ment avoids this problem: it has two elements, but the effect is monothematic and monolithic, like a great building hewn from a single slab of living rock. The third faces the problem squarely, and triumphantly – content determines a freer form, with astonish-ing results.

Like a cortège approaching through the shadows of an im-mense, vaulted cathedral nave, the slow movement emerges, *Lento espressivo e solenne,* with a dotted-note figure on timpani that is taken up by two murmuring tubas (figure *z*). Then, over a quiet F sharp drum-roll, violas and cellos give out the sombre main march-theme in bare octaves:

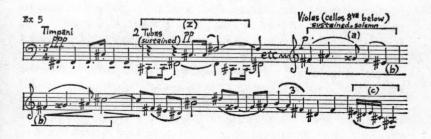

The grave, austere melody, whose tied notes and cross-rhythms so flexibly exploit the 5/4 metre, is intimately related to the pre-ceding movement, whose two subjects are echoed in its single line. The first bar (fig. *5a*) is a slight variation of *3a*, while fig. *5b* varies the basic shape (*2a*) of the symphony's opening theme. Here the opposing subjects are, in a sense, reconciled, and Brian does not now experiment with another polarisation. Instead, though figure *z* and the rest of the Ex. 5 material remain separate entities, their juxtaposition is part of one process, one inexorable momentum. The structure evolves step by step as a titanic funeral procession, built around increasingly climatic statements of the march-theme; while intervening episodes are strictly derived from the same source. Here, in this mighty *Lento* with its granitic, rock-like instrumentation, Brian has fully attained the quality of monumentality that characterises so much of his later music.

After its initial F sharp statement, the march-theme is im-mediately heard in rich harmony in G flat major on woodwind and horns, over a pizzicato even-crotchet bass, evoking march-ing footfalls. Figure z returns, burgeoning upwards in divided strings while 5*a* is passed among the woodwind. Then the tubas resume their figure, impelling the music towards the next state-ment of the march-theme. This ('becoming gradually passionate and tragic')[1] is dark and *sonore* on all bass instruments, in G flat minor; it ends with fig. 5*c* extended in a terse dialogue between high and low registers that anticipates the tough motivic play of Brian's later symphonies.

Now tubas, cellos and basses weld together figures z and 5*c* to form a sinewy bass line that strives upward in a great arch while strings and woodwind comment in passionate descending phrases. It sinks back, and in the gloom sepulchral low harp-notes sound another even-crochet pattern. The writhing bass line returns to carry the music towards a climax, in progressively rising phrases, with horns boldly to the fore. At the apex of the ascent, trombones and tubas make of the harp pattern a magisterial return into the depths, cadencing into D minor and the grandest statement of the march-theme so far. It adopts the even-crotchet rhythm, and full strings, harps, trombones and tubas proclaim it in crunching dissonance against a pulsing D from 6 horns. The mood has grown solemn, grand, and exalted. The pace slows; the 2 timpani, with all bass instruments, hammer out 5*c* in ponderous augmenta-tion; and abruptly the music enters a world of fire and ice.

The motion is suddenly much quicker. In the highest register, 4 flutes and a piccolo set up an ostinato of chittering semiquavers, while muted trumpets, harps, and pizzicato violins and violas have a biting quaver figure that is essentially a diminution of 5*a*. Far below, as in the depths of some crevasse, a new bass figure

---

[1] One of the score's many indications in English.

heaves on lowest woodwind and strings – derived from *z*, but with its characteristic fourth altered to a tritone. The orchestration strikingly anticipates a passage in Vaughan Williams's *Sinfonia Antartica*, but Brian's intention is not pictorial. These are cold, fantastic regions of the mind. A blizzard of tremolo violin tone envelops the scene for an instant, and when it clears the quaver ostinato has shifted to flutes, clarinets, and the entire oboe family; the grim bass is still heaving, and a chill whirlwind of triplet semiquaver figuration is sweeping through violins and violas.

At length we are recalled to ostensibly more objective matters by a bald brass fanfare on the tritone form of *z*, descending to a thunderous low organ pedal and timpani-roll. An angry figure erupts on trumpets and woodwind, derived from the first 3 notes of *5a*. With developments of this figure, and distorted versions of *5b* in the bass, the music mounts towards its culmination. Strings, timpani and woodwind seize on the triad of D sharp minor and, in a rictus of frenzy, hammer it out wildly until trumpets and trombones join in to force the music twice upwards towards G with thrilling effect. The second time, the march-theme crashes in, with awe-inspiring grandeur, in E flat minor. This, the climactic statement of the theme, is on organ and full orchestra, in even-crotchet rhythm, save that the 6 horns, as if dogging the steps of the main cortège, proclain the original (Ex. 5) form of the theme against it – in the original G flat major!

The splendour unabated, the music strides on to yet one more even-crotchet statement, with trumpets and pizzicato strings to the fore, in E minor: note that the three biggest statements of the theme have moved in ascending semitonal steps towards E. Trombones and tubas cadence back to the movement's home key of G flat in great swinging strides, and only now, with characteristic suddenness, does Brian dismiss the climax. Between one bar and the next the shadows fall, and we are left with the sound of the lower strings receding into quietness. Already the great procession seems to have moved very far away, almost beyond our hearing. The brief coda is a last distant echo of it. The 2 tubas, *molto sostenuto*, resume figure *z* in G flat major, as an ostinato over which 3 horns, *pppp*, *sotto voce*, slowly dissolve the opening bar of the march-theme. From their fading echoes emerges a solo bass clarinet, descending from G flat until it comes to rest on a low sustained D. Over this, the scherzo begins.

At least, the ensuing movement is generally called the 'scherzo'
of *The Gothic*, but that is to diminish its nature and misunderstand
its function. For it is both the *finale* of Part I and the immediate
prelude to the *Te Deum*. On it the whole expressive weight and
impetus of Part I must fall – and Brian has created a movement
fully worthy of that responsibility. This towering *Vivace* surpasses
the slow movement in quality by as much again as that had out-
ranked the first; and it has proved in performance to be the part
of *The Gothic* which most readily wins general admiration. Rightly
so – for it bears judgement by the very highest standards: it is
the most original thing Brian had so far composed, and announces
his maturity as a symphonist in unmistakable terms.

The movement begins quietly, in D minor, with a mysterious,
rushing, Brucknerian ostinato-figure (Ex. 6*a*) in timpani and *sul
ponticello* strings, over which a terse theme – a variant of 2*a* from
the first movement – appears on solo oboe (Ex. 6*b*). Faintly

sinister even at first hearing, 6*b* grows with frightening speed
through a host of canonic entries on woodwind and brass. A
weirdly-scored polytonal fabric rears up, in which 6*b* is distorted
in a myriad ways, its parodied shapes like gargoyles leering from
the crannies of a cathedral façade. The ostinato 6*a*, still rooted
in D minor, carries it all; and far below, uncouth in their
lowest register, the tubas play a chromatic descent of 4 long notes,
B♭ – A – G♯ – G♮.[1] All at once, edifice and ostinato vanish, and
from a new direction – F major – comes a burst of glowing horn
tone:

[1] Paul Rapoport observes that the same 4 notes appear as illustration of the
trombone 'pedal' range in Berlioz's *Traité de l'Orchestration,* which Brian knew in
the German version revised by Richard Strauss. Coincidence seems to be excluded,
especially as Brian later gives the figure to trombones; but what matters is the
highly creative use he makes of this very basic figure.

Is this a return to the dilemma of the first movement – a vigorous opening confounded by an immobile and too greatly contrasting second subject? By no means. Ex. 7 maintains thematic unity – it is a direct transformation of *6b*. Nor is it a long melody, but a self-contained unit, at once evocative and epigrammatic. The vigour has not been dissipated – the timpani ictus shows it is still there, latent. But most important, Ex. 7 is not a 'second subject': this is no sonata design, and preconceptions of form are no aid to its appreciation. Its design is unique – something we shall discover of many movements, even whole symphonies, in Brian's output. To understand it we must first experience it from point to point.

The horns reiterate Ex. 7 whose brightness soon dims into quiet mystery. The ostinato *6a* returns in the timpani, and the music moves back to D minor, the ostinato fading out on pizzicato cellos. There is a brief pause; then a new section begins, slower but still energetic, with a stormy, passionate theme over *6b* used as a canonic bass:

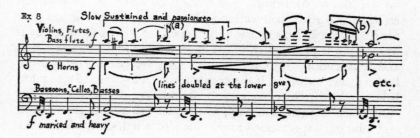

This music expands itself in gorgeous orchestration and rich, complex polyphonic working, the downward-curling semiquaver figure (*8b*) showing itself apt to all kinds of transformation. Then all at once it subsides quietly into E minor. The tempo is suddenly

Adagio, though the quick beating of a side-drum disguises the fact at first. Then enter, in the middle register, 2 harps, creating an inner pedal on E; in the lowest reaches of the bass, trombones playing the deep 'pedal' notes outside their normal range, in slow chromatic descent, B♭ – A – G♯ – G♮; and lastly, high in the treble, flutes and 2 muted violins, lingering over a scrap of theme that might derive from 8*a*. The bareness of the textures and the sense of measureless vertical space they create are remarkable.

As other woodwind enter, the harmony grows warmer and richer, but the music's essential stillness is undisturbed. Then flutes and oboes state figure 8*a* in recognizable terms; it is taken up, dreamily, by high violins and violas; and far below, the trombones again have their solemn 4-note descent. Without warning, a new, bright *Allegro* bursts in, in C flat.

All this might seem to some a disconcertingly formless kind of procedure. So far we have heard four very diverse passages; now here is a fifth, yet no hint of symmetry has emerged: what is the form, and what function do these sections have in it? In fact each partakes a little of exposition, development, and episode at once. They do 'expose' thematic material. 'Development' has been under way, however obliquely, from the first. But each section remains an 'episode' – none can take over completely, as did the second subject in the first movement. As they alternate, their various tempi hint that they are simply different aspects of some larger, hidden momentum which is never broken. Brian is familiarising us with the idea that contrasts may be yoked together *without* loss of continuity, and though he does for the moment maintain thematic connections, they are noticeably loose. For continuity in Brian's music lies deeper than themes or keys: it lies as deep as personality, in the momentum generated by passion and imagination. Such symphonism may be 'open' in form, but by no means formless, if the composer has the sense of structural balance that Brian possesses in abundance. These preliminary sections have been necessary, to suggest the overall momentum and raise our expectations to the required pitch. Only *now* can the music drive ahead.

The new *Allegro* tempo ('much faster free and bright') does so with splashing chords on woodwind, harps and triangle, and trumpets blazoning forth a crisp fanfare, before the music shifts to E flat minor and plunges into what is, in effect, a vivacious development section. It moves from discussion of 8a to 6b and 8b, and slows momentarily for an impassioned statement of these two combined into one sweeping melody. A tensely chromatic variation of 6b on violas and flutes leads to further development in A minor before the storm calms in the direction of F.

At this point the distant horn fanfare, Ex. 7, returns. Though not unaltered from its first appearance (it is stated over a pedal D from bassoons, cellos, horns and basses, and punctuated by chiming harps and glockenspiel), it is the nearest thing to a literal repetition we have yet encountered, and is plainly a structural landmark. In fact, it signals the mid-point of the movement; and here, at the geographical centre, we find an extraordinary thing. There are two statements of Ex. 7, and between them lies an enormously impressive structure. For a mere dozen bars, we hear a hypnotic motion of massive chords on 6 horns and bassoons, circling away from and back to D, over a repeated even-crotchet pattern in tubas, double-bassoon, cellos and basses that curves downwards from A to D and back again. Words cannot give the flavour of the thing: it is like the majestic rotation of a planet. It has a looming, elemental quality – as if a veil has been lifted to allow us a brief glimpse of the mighty engine, that 'larger momentum' that powers the movement and the symphony as a whole. Brian marks the passage 'Slow', but so inexorable is its progression that the adjective seems meaningless. Does the world turn 'slowly' on its axis? Does it orbit 'slowly' round the Sun? Again and again in Brian's music we shall find similar moments of revelation, of forces at work beneath the music's surface.

The horns return with Ex. 7, stated over a bass drum roll. That swells to a roar, and the timpani suddenly batter out a terse tonic-dominant figure (Ex. 9a). From this point onwards, the music grows a little wild.

We might describe what ensues as another development section, had we heard most of its material before. It is a furious explosion of orchestral power, *Allegro assai e con fuoco*, on entirely fresh themes, and we must get our bearings in it as best we may – though we understand it best if we allow its wild sweep to carry us along. Such is the force of the 'larger momentum' Brian has built up that this explosion seems logical and thrilling, absolutely essential to the movement's accumulating tension.

The music here is hectic and fantastically scored, with squealing

flutes, timpani like gunfire, and violins screaming in rapid semitone oscillations at the top of their register. The timpani figure
(9*a*) spawns a brusque theme (9*b*), taken up in turn by piccolo,
cornet, horns, and trumpets; and soon the horns have another,
almost jaunty, scrap of tune (9*c*): all stem ultimately from 6*a*.

Beginning around D minor, the music quickly moves away from
that key; but it soon thunders back, in a towering passion, into
a heroic march-like episode, introducing new material

but combined with 9*a* as an ostinato in the timpani, and the 4-note
chromatic descent in the trombones! The 'march' sweeps on, its
momentum apparently irresistible, through a recall of 9*c* (horns)
and a restatement of Ex. 10; and then, at the very height of the
tumult, begins one of the weirdest passages in English music.
    The mighty sounds of the full orchestra are suddenly extin-
guished in mid-phrase, to be replaced by a thin high whine of
densely-clustered violin harmonics. Beneath this eerie sound,

harps and cellos, their rhythm pointed up by the side-drum, thrum continuous quaver chords of C sharp minor. The tubas enter with a low ominous theme which recalls the opening of Schubert's *Unfinished* Symphony, yet in this orchestration sounds strange and saurian. Flutes and piccolos chitter into life; and with an upward-swooping glissando and a crash, a solo xylophone invades the scene. Its macabre rattle and grotesque dotted rhythms cut through the accumulating textures as it launches into a fiercely virtuosic fantasia. The timpanists, playing 4 drums, enter to reinforce the C sharp minor chords, and the music is convulsed by squealing runs (almost glissandi) in the treble instruments and snarling ones in the bass. The whining harmonics have never ceased, however; the music settles back into C sharp, the thrummed chords now in cellos, basses and timpani, supported by gong and organ pedal. The xylophone combines with the flutes and piccolos in a skirling ostinato of sextuplet semiquavers.[1]

The music seems possessed by an uncanny rictus: it is racing ahead, flat out, and yet the effect is absolutely static – just as the Earth rushes through space at unimaginable speed, yet seems to us not to be moving at all. The idea of *tempo* has disappeared, because harmonic movement has ceased, and every passing second screws the tension to a higher pitch.

The 4 drums switch to a triad of B flat, while C sharp persists in the rest of the orchestra. By now, 10 of the 12 notes of the chromatic scale are being continually sounded: only G and C are lacking. And then, with awesome effect, trombones and tubas blast their way through the fabric with the 4-note descent, and they alone precipitate harmonic movement. They enter on a low B♭, and with huge deliberation move downwards to A, to G♯, and finally to G♮, which swells in a great crescendo until the accumulated tension can no longer be contained. Only C is now missing. G becomes a dominant, and the music plunges, with both

[1] I know of no parallel to this extraordinary episode in any other composer's music. In Brian's own output it is foreshadowed, though in much less extreme form, in the similarly-scored *Allegro alla Marcia* section of the Symphonic Dance *Gargoyles* from *The Tigers*. Brian's xylophone writing, so characteristic a feature of his music, is wholly individual. It is difficult to imagine what inspired it: possibly the pre-War music-halls, where many instrumentalists did 'star turns' of remarkable virtuosity, may have featured some bravura xylophone acts.

tonal and a kind of 'serial' logic, into C minor, and the climax
that Brian has so brilliantly prepared.

The music heaves like a plain on which great armies are
embattled. Side-drum and upper woodwind beat out a martial,
pounding rhythm[1] against which strings play a tough ostinato
deriving from 6*a*. Bassoons and tubas make a bass of the 'saurian'
theme in altered rhythm, while the rest of the brass have the lions'
share of glory in a vast series of canonic entries combining 6*b*
with 8*b*. Trumpets and cornets ring out proudly above the storm,
with a note of victory, a sense of triumph and exultation that must
have been Brian's own as he came to the end of this superb
movement. The music soars in boundless confidence; harps,
xylophone and organ enter with more ostinati; and suddenly – it
is the climax of Part I – Brian flings the music back into its home
key of D minor with a cadence of astonishing boldness:

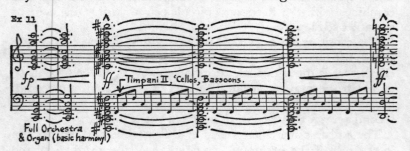

From C major to D minor by way of F sharp, all in three
triads: it is the sensational juxtaposition of C and F sharp that is
so exhilarating. Brian has discovered his full powers. He can
stride from one end of the tonal universe to the other in a split
second: he can make a single cadence bear the dramatic weight of
an entire movement. This is the victory of imagination over form.

Back in D minor, the music rises to a pinnacle of grandeur,
with 6*a* returning as an ostinato on strings and organ, and final
canonic entries on 6*b*, before all instruments hammer home the
chord of D, faster and faster, *fff*, only to be shut off with heart-
stopping suddenness. There is a pause, then quietness – a high
tremolo in the violins, a soft meditative glow from the bassoons,
6*a* barely audible in the timpani to assure us that the world is still

---

[1] Very similar to the drum-rhythm of the 'battle' scene in *Ein Heldenleben* which
Brian had already brilliantly parodied in Act II of *The Tigers*.

spinning. A solo horn, reminiscently, winds 9c. Then for the last time the distant fanfare, Ex. 7, echoes over the plains. A calm series of woodwind chords (not unrelated to the 'turning world' music, about which, in retrospect, the entire movement seems to have hinged) ascends through the space of 8 bars; and Part I of *The Gothic* ends in a serenely-spaced D major triad,[1] adorned with harp arpeggios, on a very high plateau of achievement indeed.

PART II

1. *Te Deum laudamus*   2. *Judex crederis esse venturus*
3. *Te ergo quaesumus*

Ideally, the work is continuous: the serene triad fades away, and for the first time in the symphony the human voice is heard as *a capella* children's and women's choirs burst into radiant song with the opening words of the *Te Deum*. By dint of the strivings in Part I we have, it seems, attained a kind of grace: now we are vouchsafed a vision.

It is a heady, even hallucinatory vision, and to convey it Brian employs those mighty forces which have raised *The Gothic* to the realms of the fabulous. Ignoring the inaccurate (and usually-cited) list on the flyleaf, the score requires, if taken literally, the following colossal orchestra (including doublings): 2 piccolos, 6 flutes, alto flute, 6 oboes, oboe d'amore, bass oboe, 2 cors anglais, 2 E-flat clarinets, 5 B-flat clarinets, 2 bassett-horns, 2 bass clarinets, pedal clarinet, 3 bassoons, 2 double bassoons, 8 horns, 2 E-flat cornets, 8 trumpets, bass trumpet, 3 tenor, 1 bass and 2 contrabass trombones, 2 euphoniums, 2 tubas, 2 sets of timpani, 2 harps, organ, celesta, glockenspiel, xylophone, 2 bass drums, 2 side-drums, 1 (African) long drum, 2 tambourines, 6 large pairs of cymbals, gong, thunder-machine, tubular bells, chimes, small chains, 2 triangles, bird scare, a body of strings to match, soprano, alto, tenor and bass soloists, 2 large double choruses, children's chorus, and 4 extra brass bands, equally constituted and adding

---

[1] Both the autograph and the printed score show an added sixth, supplied by a B in the 5th horn. However, during rehearsals for the 1966 performance the composer decided to substitute an A, making the whole chord a simple triad. The effect is chaster and more logical.

to the total a further 8 horns, 8 trumpets, 8 tenor trombones, 8 tubas and 4 sets of timpani.[1]

With these unheard-of resources, Brian in the *Te Deum* constructs a huge, labyrinthine structure which largely renounces traditional thematically-based architectural principles. It is as if he were intent on testing his mastery of form to the limit in the most extreme circumstances and with the most diverse materials. The result is less like a late-Romantic effusion than some complex marvel of Renaissance polyphony: one thinks of Tallis's great 40-part motet, *Spem in Alium*, pushing part-writing to its imaginable limits in a fashion comparable to Brian's treatment of solo voices, choirs, bands and orchestra.

In fact the *Te Deum* seems in a curious way to stand outside time, a fantastic synthesis, at many levels, of different ages of music. Apart from a strong modal feeling, there is nothing specifically archaic about the style – indeed it is notably 'advanced' for an English composer writing in the early 1920's. The huge orchestra outdoes Mahler and Schoenberg; the massed choral forces belong to the imaginative world of the great pre-War choir festivals. Yet somehow they seem to pick up and amplify the resonances of past centuries. Brian himself pointed out that the *Te Deum* belonged as much to the world of Palestrina and Byrd as to *Tristan*; its organum, modality and free verbal accentuation are mediaeval in effect; the spatial disposition of forces at times resembles that of Giovanni Gabrieli; the long, florid, melismatic vocal lines recall the great pre-Reformation Tudor composers, such as Taverner and Fairfax; in chromatic freedom the harmony rivals Gesualdo. Yet the music owes little directly to any of these influences; in sum it is a profoundly original creative achievement, which speaks with the recognizable voice of our own century.

Of course it is not uniformly successful. Its complexity and lack of conventional thematic articulation (of which more later) make it hard to grasp at first, and often there is almost too much for the

---

[1] So far in performance the brass bands have been reduced to two, but this is not ideal in view of the spatial conception of the whole. If possible, the four half-choirs should be ranged in a vast semi-circle above and behind the orchestra, each with a brass orchestra behind *it*. The orchestral trumpets could be reduced to 4, and the second contra-bass trombone can be dispensed with. The 'thunder-machine' is the German *Donnermaschine* (as used in Strauss's *Alpine Symphony*), and *not* the thunder-*sheet* which has been employed so far. Owing to a printing error, neither this nor the long drum actually appear in the score – but they are used in the final climax, co-extensively with the bird-scare.

ear to take in. At some points, myriads of notes seem to be required for some fairly unsensational effects. But given the immensity of what Brian was trying to do, the wonder is that his success was so nearly complete. There are scores of instances where the vast forces justify themselves by securing effects of richness, power and beauty that could be gained in no other way. And the piece has an enormous sense of occasion: a performance of it will always be an event, for the size and splendour of the overall conception almost beggars parallel.

Let us look first at the *a capella* opening.

Te Deum laudamus: te Dominum confitemur

The main theme, in the children's voices, varies the rising triadic shape that had dominated Part I (12a). The flattened 7th (C) strongly suggests a modal colouring, though the female-voice faux-bourdon confirms that the key is D major. After the initial statement by high voices, the solo quartet enter in 4-part counterpoint, the soprano singing the main melody; then the women and children join them in more chant-like lines, ending on a bare-fifth chord of D.

2 horns are heard calling in quiet canon; then 4, louder, more martial; and the whole orchestra comes to life in a superb D major fanfare, with trumpets to the fore. Only when it has ended does the full splendour of the *Te Deum* burst upon us, *Allegro molto e con*

brio. While first the basses of both choirs, then the children's choir, sing the main theme of Ex. 12 in canon with various parts of the orchestra, the other voices and instruments have multiple subsidiary canons either on fragments of the theme (especially 12*a* and *b*), or decorated variations of it – all overlapping to create a jangling, jubilant, bell-like heterophony in a dozen or more simultaneous contrapuntal lines.

Te aeternum Patrem omnis terra veneratur.
Tibi omnes Angeli, tibi Coeli et universae potestates.

The key changes to B major, and the full choirs intone 'Te aeternum Patrem . . .' against a massive 2-part canon on 12*a* in full brass; then for 'Tibi omnes Angeli . . .' the music quietens and the choirs divide into 12 parts, with the main theme gently stated in divided strings – for the last time.

So far the thematic thread provided by Ex. 12 has been easy to follow; but from now on Brian abjures thematic working almost entirely. This is not to say there are no recognizable tunes: there are scores of them. But they often appear no more than once; are not developed in any way; and at best have merely 'local' significance. They are the passing manifestations of a free-wheeling, untrammelled, and inexhaustibly fertile process of invention. There is nothing arbitrary about their use – Brian really is conducting a powerful symphonic argument over an enormous time-scale: it is just that melodic shapes have become auxiliaries to, rather than the substance of, that argument.

Seven typical melodies from the *Te Deum* are set out in Ex. 13, and the main theme of Ex. 12 could be added to their number. These and many like them occur in different contexts, in widely separated regions of the vast structure. They are not 'developments' one from another in the orthodox meaning of the term. Nevertheless, they are not unrelated. Each has some or all of the following characteristics:

(1) They are long melodies (generally unusual in Brian's music, but very characteristic of the *Te Deum*), mostly with a wide range of up to 2 octaves.

(2) They display various degrees of rhythmic freedom, often ignoring the stresses of bar-lines, and producing cross-rhythms through triplet formations.

(3) They vary the rising triadic shape from Part I, often modify-

45

Ex 13

ing it into an augmented triad. (Harmonically, the augmented triad is the most important single agent of tonal ambiguity throughout the *Te Deum*). Even when the whole shape is not present, the interval of a rising 6th is equally important.

Thus these melodies, though not the subjects of *thematic* development, are members of 'families' which contribute to the overall *stylistic* unity-in-diversity of the *Te Deum*, allowing the music to impose a logic that can be sensed, if not always explained.

> *Tibi cherubim et seraphim incessabili voce proclamant,*
> *Sanctus, sanctus, sanctus, Dominus Deus Sabaoth.*

The female voices break in with various canonic fragments to the words, accompanied chiefly by the 'angelic' sounds of flutes, harps, glockenspiel, violins, and organ (voix celeste). Soon they pass into a flowing 4-part canonic chorus of 'Sanctus', then divide into 8, with children's voices chanting a ninth part. Their role becomes increasingly important while the orchestration grows ever more glittering, with triplet semiquaver ostinati in 2 piccolos, 4 flutes, xylophone and glockenspiel, plus theme (*i*) from Ex. 13 in the strings. Tenors and basses enter to swell the growing chorus, and the passage reaches a great climax, marked 'Stately and Majestic' on 'Dominus Deus . . .'. Here soloists, choirs and children combine in 14-part polyphony against full orchestra, with pealing carillon-like figures on tubular bells, harps, glockenspiel, xylophone, and pizzicato strings.

> *Pleni sunt coeli et terra majestatis gloriae tuae.*
> *Te gloriosus Apostolorum chorus,*
> *Te prophetarum laudabilis numerus,*
> *Te Martyrum candidatus laudat exercitus*
>   *(Dominus Deus Sabaoth)*
> *Te per orbem terrarum sancta confitemur Ecclesia.*

Abruptly the character of the music changes. First male and then female choruses sing chant-like melodies against striding march-rhythms in bassoons and timpani, coming together (with the children's choir) for the repetition of 'Dominus Deus Sabaoth'. A short, solemn fanfare for brass and organ now takes the music – for the first time since the *Te Deum* began – into E major, and the choirs sing various unaccompanied settings of 'Te per orbem . . .' in slow 8-part and 12-part polyphony.

> *Patrem immensae majestatis,*
> *Venerandum tuum verum et unicum filium,*
> *Sanctum quoque paracletum Spiritum.*

The orchestra re-enters and the pace quickens, the music being carried onward by rising 3-note figures in bass voices and instruments. The passage reaches a richly contrapuntal climax on A flat with 'Paracletum Spiritum', and subsides into C. The key becomes D flat, and there is a magically beautiful moment as soft, evocative trumpet-calls sound through tranquil chords on muted strings. Their rhythm becomes all-pervasive, and the strings and trumpets accelerate into a fierce fanfare, rapidly modulating to D major and announcing a fortissimo outburst from the full choirs.

> *Tu Rex Gloriae Christe,*
> *Tu Patris sempiternus es Filius.*

After two unaccompanied statements of the first line, the choirs join the orchestra in another pealing, many-voiced canon. It is short-lived, however, and breaks off to leave the voices reiterating 'Christe' against sustained oboe chords and a weird, curving phrase on solo euphonium. Another slow quiet unaccompanied passage swings the music round to E again, with some very chromatic choral writing.

> *Tu ad liberandum suscepturus hominem,*
> *non horruisti Virginis uterum.*
> *Tu devicto mortis aculeo, aperuisti credentibus*
> *Regna coelorum.*

The music is still *a capella*. 'Tu ad liberandum . . .' and 'Tu devicto . . .' are set as syllabic chanting in A minor, but they frame a remarkable E major setting of 'Non horruisti . . .' as a strict 4-part canon on an extremely chromatic theme. It serves as a good illustration of the uncompromising nature of Brian's vocal writing:

A fortissimo repetition of 'Tu devicto . . .' leads to the key of F sharp and the final section of the movement.

> *Tu ad dexteram Dei sedes, in gloria Patris.*

This begins *Moderato Allegro mais brio molto* as a jubilant outburst for full choirs and orchestra, with plenty of the customary canonic

writing. But the music quietens as it moves into E flat minor, with
the choirs accompanied by euphoniums and tubas. As jubilation
returns, however, the key becomes E flat *major*, and the music
less contrapuntal, more massively grand. Eventually, it strides
forward confidently into E major, and that key brings a brief but
blazing climax on 'Gloria', with elating trumpets prominent
amid the vast *tutti*. The final word 'Patrem', however, brings an
awe-struck hush and a long-drawn-out phrase suggesting the
minor key, until in the very last bar the movement concludes on a
pianissimo triad of E major. Thus the first section of Part II, after
several moves in that direction, has established E as the new tonal
centre of the symphony, fulfilling the tendency of Part I. Now,
for the rest of the work, E is often challenged by its relative C
sharp minor.

The second movement of Part II uses only 4 words of the Latin
text: *Judex crederis esse venturus* – 'We believe Thou shalt come to
be our Judge' – and, in contrast to the brightness of the preceding
movement, the thought of judgement and an inevitable end brings
music of almost unrelieved tension. It opens in E, but E minor;
and after announcing the first word, the female voices sing it in
superimposed triads of D minor, E minor, G major and A minor,
creating a 'cluster' chord of vibrant dissonance.

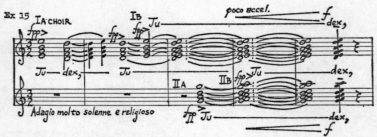

The male voices repeat the passage, and then the solo soprano
sings the words to a long, floating, melismatic line. The choruses
resume in a complex 16-part texture made up of canons on a rising
triadic theme, free contrapuntal lines, and accompanying chords
of triads and inversions. They divide further, into 20 parts, the
female voices singing 'Judex' in overlapping triads of G minor
and F minor, with a further canon in the tenor voices and a stream

of triads in remote keys from the basses. The tonality veers to E flat, but eventually this highly dissonant, chromatic passage ends on a bare-fifth of A. The solo soprano takes over on a high A, sounding as if from afar, singing a serene vocalise. As it dies into inaudibility, the 8 trumpets of the brass bands suddenly leap into action, like tongues of flame, with a brilliant, fiercely virtuosic canonic fanfare. They climax on a swelling chord of C sharp, whereupon a solo horn reiterates the final part of the soprano's vocalise.

Now begins a substantial interlude for orchestra alone, *Andante ma pesante*. It does not develop previous material except, in the allusive fashion of this *Te Deum*, by introducing melodies *similar* to what has passed before. Its chief focus of activity is a gruff figure of 4 quavers, heard especially in euphoniums and tubas. Its mood is grim, heavy, and processional. Eventually it reaches a tumultuous climax on an augmented triad of A flat, with a wild fanfare for trumpets and side-drum. There is a dramatic pause, and then, in turn, each of the 4 choruses, supported by its own complete brass orchestra and timpani, proclaims 'Judex crederis esse venturus'. Were it possible to distribute the forces as Brian envisaged, the effect would be of the music wheeling round in a great half-circle. All four statements are different, though similar in character; and between them strings and woodwind play three long-spanned melodies – quite different from the choral passages but, again, similar to each other (theme *ii* from Ex. 13 is the second of them). The whole section circles through keys as well: the first choral statement is in F minor, and the last leads to the re-entry of the full orchestra in C sharp.

This second big orchestral interlude is faster, more delicately scored, and lighter in tone than the first. Horns soon introduce an optimistic theme (*iii* from Ex. 13) and Brian proceeds to press many similar melodies into service, culminating at length in a bold, brassy climax. After that the tempo slows, the mood darkens, and the voices enter, one section at a time, over a timpani ostinato. The key is again E minor, but the music moves steadily away from it, with complex overlapping vocal entries, flutter-tongue writing in the flutes, and rapidly-changing harp figurations. It reaches C sharp minor, at which point the brass orchestras enter to swell the sound and texture; then G sharp minor – and an enormous climax is unleashed. This is one of the rare occasions in the *Te Deum* where almost the full forces are heard together at maximum volume. It culminates in rising choral cries against multiple orchestral ostinati; 3 bars of massive modulatory chords for woodwind, strings, harps, and 32 brass; and a final apocalyptic establishment of E major for the entire forces (with 56 brass and 6 sets of timpani), more terrifying than triumphant, the whole gigantic sound topped off by the bird-scare's demonic whirring.

The third and final movement of the *Te Deum* is also the longest, the most varied in musical character, and the one showing the greatest range of vocal and instrumental resources. Even thematic development of a more familiar kind is allowed to operate in places. It opens with a long, calm melody for unaccompanied oboe d'amore (*iv* from Ex. 13), which introduces an extended aria for the tenor soloist.

> *Te ergo quaesumus tuis famulis subveni,*
> *quos pretioso sanguine redemisti.*

The music never strays far from the key of C sharp minor. The writing for the solo voice is floridly elaborate and long-breathed, with syllables extended in long, ornate phrases; the mood is impassioned, supplicatory, yet exalted. Brian first accompanies the voice in delicate textures of tremolo strings, woodwind, solo string instruments – at one point a solo string quartet is brought into prominence. Later, as the brass develop the figure *a* from theme *iv*, the texture thickens and the aria reaches a dramatic, almost operatic climax, with the tenor pitted against full orchestra. When the tension relaxes, the key changes to A major, and against a high tremolo in the violins a solo cor anglais states a melody similar to theme *iv*. Then that theme itself is recalled, serenely, in the cellos' highest register, beneath a crystalline, 9-part texture of tremolo violins and violas.

> *Aeterna fac cum sanctis tuis in gloria numerari.*

The tenor re-enters, *Andante religioso*, to sing these words against calm woodwind chords and pizzicato strings. There is a pause, and then the first violins steal in with a quiet *Molto vivace* idea that initiates a swift-winged Allegro.

The textures remain light and airy, with important parts for solo violin and viola. The female voices enter, singing rising augmented-triad figures to the vowel 'Ah'; and the music sweeps into a confident E major. Now the solo soprano has a brief but heady rendering of the words, accompanied by gay figuration derived from Ex. 16 in harps and pizzicato violins. The celestial dance continues for a while in orchestra alone, before the choirs begin to join in. Steadily the music grows in complexity as more and more voices enter, with two solo violins soaring high above the accumulating polyphonic lines. Rhythmically and texturally this is perhaps the densest part of the entire symphony, but Brian maintains a firm sense of ebullient forward motion. Theme *v* from Ex. 13 enters in the bass in C sharp major; the orchestration grows fuller; the choirs divide into 16 parts; the words shrink to repetitions of 'gloria numerari' – not quite a grammatical unit, but suggesting in this context that 'It is glorious to be numerous'! Eventually, the whole vast flood of music reaches a superb A major climax as bass trumpet, trombones, euphoniums and tubas proclaim theme *vi* of Ex. 13 in triumph. The female voices softly sing a last 'Aeterna . . .', and then the male voices strike in, unaccompanied.

Salvum fac populum tuum, Domine.

This is another substantial *a capella* episode, for tenors and basses only, much divided. Long, elaborate phrases, including tenor and bass solos from within the choirs, are interspersed with syllabic chanting that gradually grows more urgent (repetitions of 'Domine! Domine!') until all the voices combine in a dissonant fortissimo chant of the whole line. On the last syllable, female voices and orchestra take over.

Et benedic haereditate tuae.

Again the music is joyous, the high voices accompanied by high woodwind and important repeated-note figures on harps, xylophone and pizzicato strings. From these figures springs a lively trumpet obbligato, against whose silver tones the sopranos and contraltos vocalise to 'Ah'. For a moment, the music seems to have strayed into that magical region which, 30 years later, Michael Tippett was to explore in *The Midsummer Marriage*.

> *Et rege eos et extolle usque in aeternum.*
> *Per singulos dies benedicimus te.*

Tenors, basses and organ enter, *Andante moderato*, in a grand E major rendering of 'Et rege eos . . .', soon supported by full brass. The women's voices take over the words against harps and woodwind; and then the children's choir – girls and boys in 2-part counterpoint – join in with a smoothly flowing tune for 'Per singulos dies . . .'. The solo vocal quartet repeat the first line; and the choirs repeat the second over a quiet drum-rhythm.

Now comes a complete change of mood. The drum-rhythm becomes a steady beat on cymbals, bass drum and side-drum; and 5 clarinets, 2 bass clarinets and 2 bassett-horns begin a jaunty march-tune in A minor (Ex. 17*a*). The obviousness and simple aplomb of the material and complete absence of counterpoint are in marked contrast to the style of 'gloria numerari'. But, as we know from Bruckner and Mahler, a primitive – which is to say, elemental – simplicity has a real place in heavenly visions.

Ex 17 **Allegro Moderato**
(a) Clarinets a 5, bass cls. & bassett-hns. 8ᵛᵉ lower.

(b) CHOIRS in 8ᵛᵉˢ. ('La')

(c) Et laud—a—mus no-men tu-um in sae—cu—lum
CHOIRS & Brass in 8ᵛᵉˢ.

One by one, the voices and sections of the orchestra enter quietly, the singers vocalising in the spirit of the march-tune. The

key becomes familiar E major, and over a timpani ostinato and
echoing horns (one directed to 'sound like a posthorn' – very
Mahlerian, this!) the choirs sing an innocent, childlike tune (Ex.
17*b*), obviously related to 17*a* and, more distantly, to Ex. 12 and
some of the themes of Ex. 13. They continue tranquilly for a little;
then an outburst by 8 horns and 2 sets of timpani spurs the music,
Vivace brillante, into an almost cosmic rejoicing.

> *Et laudamus nomen tuum in saeculum saeculi.*

There is nothing obscure about this section, with its march-
rhythms, its elating tunes, its brassy virulence, its firm tonal
grounding in E Major. Yet its simplicities are writ so large (and
loud) that they somehow attain a kind of sublimity. Mahler is
insufficient comparison: here, one thinks rather of Beethoven.
Brian cunningly intercuts his tutti outbursts (mainly on Ex. 17*c*,
a rhythmic variation of the childlike 17*b*) with brief quieter
episodes – one featuring a gay E-flat clarinet solo accompanied by
vibrating small chains, another a nonchalant transformation of
17*c* on solo horn. At the roof-raising climax, the 4 brass bands
enter, and the entire forces hammer out an E major triad to the
simplest rhythms imaginable. Then at once choirs, organ and
harps modulate softly back to A minor, and the clarinet march is
heard again, as a kind of 'recessional'.

From this vision of joy, however, the music now turns to less
comforting Last Things, and steadily becomes more anguished,
more expressive of individual, subjective fears.

> *Dignare, Domine, die isto, sine peccato nos custodire.*
> *Miserere nostri, Domine.*

The bass soloist enters with an aria to these words, calm at first
but becoming more agitated; the orchestra accompanies in irregul-
arly throbbing rhythms and there is a C sharp minor climax, the
soloist's voice being overwhelmed by trombones, gong, and
flutter-tongue trumpets. The music slows, *Adagio doloroso*, and the
full brass state what sounds like the opening phrase of some
awesome chorale. The bass soloist intones 'Fiat misericordia tua
Domine super nos'; then, on a high E, 'quemadmodum spera-
vimus in te'. Taking up his last words, the choirs softly begin
what proves to be a double-fugue exposition of deeply moving
simplicity, to 'In te, Domine speravi'. Its upper theme makes

clear reference to the rising triadic shape of the symphony's opening.

This flowers into one of Brian's finest and most touching examples of *a capella* contrapuntal writing. But it is not dwelt on over-long: it makes a profoundly affecting cadence into a long-held triad of E minor on 'Domine', while the orchestra sadly plays the counter-theme of Ex. 18. Why so affecting? Perhaps because, in this vast work of modal scales, harmonic ambiguity, and plagal cadences, this is one of the few unsullied 'authentic' cadences to be found. But now, as it dies, all hell breaks loose.

One by one, the 6 timpanists, using 18 drums, enter, super-imposing several conflicting rhythms – at first quietly menacing, but increasing in volume every second. Two bass drummers join in; and soon the whole huge brass section of combined bands and orchestra comes to life in a malevolent cacophony of flutter-tonguing and jagged downward-thrusting figures. There is a fateful tolling of deep bells; and suddenly full brass, percussion, organ and thunder-machine climax in a chord of C sharp minor and the choirs give out a dissonant cry of 'Non confundar!' The 18 drums resume, their rhythms now more motoric and irresist-ible; there is another, quicker build-up, with cornets shrieking at the top of their register; another huge chord (of E minor) and an agonised 'Non confundar in aeternum' from the choirs. Then a stark fanfare in the orchestral brass culminates in an enormous, grinding E minor appoggiatura for full forces, dying away to be pianissimo.

All that now remains of the climactic appoggiatura is a high tremolo E on the violins, far beneath which a single set of timpani states a rising minor third, harking back to the very beginning of the symphony. A pause: and then the cellos, unaccompanied, sing out passionately in a long 'speaking' melody (theme *vii* from Ex. 13). The effect is of a cry *de profundis*: like the anguished viola

theme which opens Mahler's Tenth Symphony, or the fragmentary cello 'Victima Paschali' that accompanies John Taverner's
cry 'from the lowest dungeon' in Maxwell Davies's opera. The
orchestra stirs into one last convulsive C sharp minor chord
which tails off in a mournful oboe solo. The cellos are heard
again, reaching upwards by a minor third, but, not completing
the rising triad shape, they sink down as if exhausted. Silence. And
then, out of the midst of the darkness, comes a last *a capella* murmur of voices – in E *major*, as if to suggest the possibility of a
salvation beyond despair.

So this mighty creation ends, not in triumph, but with a prayer –
among other things for the continuance of the creative power.
Thirty-one more symphonies were the answer to that prayer, and
one feels that without the experience of *The Gothic* they would
never have been possible. As Brian's boldest stride into the unknown, it profoundly moves the hearer by its sense of risking all
for the realisation of a personal vision. This heaven-storming, all-
or-nothing quality is shared by very few works of this century:
one might mention, for the nearest comparison, Schoenberg's
Jacob's Ladder and Tippett's *The Vision of St. Augustine*. In such
works as these, formal perfection is beside the point: it is the
intensity of the vision that matters. *The Gothic* – whose imper-
fections are obvious enough – may not be Havergal Brian's
greatest work, but one cannot help feeling that it is one of the
handful of creative achievements by which posterity will seek to
judge our century, and know us.

4 Symphony No. 2 in E minor (1930–31)

1. *Adagio Solenne – Allegro Assai*   2. *Andante Sostenuto*
3. *Allegro Assai*   4. *Lento Maestoso e Mesto*

For 3 years after completing *The Gothic*, Brian composed nothing except to finish the long-delayed orchestration of *The Tigers*. But in June 1930 he began to sketch a purely orchestral symphony, a large-scale work in 4 movements, which ushered in 7 years of sustained creative effort during which some of his finest works were written. However ignored he might be as a composer, he was at the height of his powers, and the writing of the Second Symphony and its immediate successors fell within one of the most stimulating periods of his life. In 1928 he had met Schoenberg; in 1932 he met Tovey and became friendly with Fritz Busch, who was eager to mount a production of *The Tigers* in Dresden. During the actual composition of Symphony No. 2 he met Paul Robeson and was much in the company of well-known people in the organ world, while many of his evenings were spent at the Savoy Hotel, yarning with the aged John Philip Sousa.

In the summer of 1930, Brian's wife and children went on holiday, leaving the composer in peace to commit his ideas to paper. He found his surroundings conducive to creative work: the house in Upper Norwood was quiet and secluded, and his study looked directly into an old wood – perhaps the last remnant of the ancient Sydenham Forest. In the other direction lay Crystal Palace, near enough for the pedal-notes of its great organ to cause a soft vibration throughout the house.

The symphony was sketched between June and September 1, the second movement actually being first in order of composition. On November 2 Brian began the full score, and completed it on April 6, 1931. For the next few years this was his working routine – rapid sketching of a new piece, mainly during the summer

Symphony No. 2: a page from the manuscript (Scherzo)

months, followed by revision and the laborious preparation of a
full score throughout the rest of the year. At the time of its completion, the Second was jocularly referred to as the 'little' Symphony, not that it was small in itself, but simply because it was so
much shorter than *The Gothic*; and like *The Gothic*, it was assigned
to Cranz. However, although advertised in their catalogues, the
work was never printed and, at the time of writing, has never
been performed.[1]

The Second Symphony raises the vexed question of 'literary
influence' in Brian's work. When Reginald Nettel was researching
for his biography of Brian, the composer explained that Symphony
No. 2 was inspired by Goethe's drama *Götz von Berlichingen*. The
four movements were associated in his mind with various aspects
of Götz's character: his ambitions, his loves, his battles, and death.
Towards the end of his life, however, Brian disclaimed this attri-
bution, and made clear that he wished all his works to be treated
as pure music, 'just like Brahms's symphonies'. His change of
attitude surely reflects anxiety lest those works with a known
inspiration in literature be vulnerable to facile misinterpretation
from people who look no further in music than for a 'programme'.
Brian never wrote programme music in that sense. His symphonies
demonstrate his mastery at the highest and most sophisticated
level of purely musical invention. Undoubtedly Romantic literature was one of the great passions of his life (especially Goethe,
Blake, and Shelley), and presumably *Götz von Berlichingen* was much
in his mind at the time of writing Symphony No. 2. But the
influence of a specific play or poem on Brian's imagination was
always that of a *catalyst*; thus, though literary associations help
fill in the background to certain works, they are best forgotten
entirely once discussion of the music starts: Brian's symphonies
need no literary prop. For instance, the finale of Symphony No. 2
is a funereal march, but that expressive image is common to many
works – a characteristic of Brian's cast of musical mind, which we
have met already in *The Gothic*. And the 'battle' scherzo, astonishing movement though it is, bears little resemblance to naturalistic
representations such as the battle-sequence in Strauss's *Ein
Heldenleben*, and must be considered on its own terms. In his last
years Brian was fond of referring to No. 2 as 'Man in his cosmic
loneliness' – a description that invites no further elaboration, while

See Appendices II and III.

indicating the tragic atmosphere that pervades the whole work.

The work is scored for a large orchestra, though a modest one compared to Part II of *The Gothic*. The first two movements employ an orchestra of quadruple woodwind (including 2 piccolos, 2 cors anglais and 2 bass clarinets), 6 horns, 4 trumpets, 4 trombones, 2 tubas, 2 harps, strings, and a percussion section including 3 sets of timpani (9 drums). In the scherzo and finale, however, 2 pianos and an organ are called for, as well as a further 10 horns – raising the total to 16, arranged in 4 groups of 4.[1]

The work displays a definite shift of style away from the more extravagant aspects of *The Gothic*, though it obviously owes much to the experience of the earlier work. There is a new concision, even terseness, in the material and its handling. Also 3 of the 4 movements are structurally very free, conforming to no orthodox pattern. The orchestral style, however, has increased in complexity, characterised by a multitude of polyphonically interweaving inner lines. The division of the strings into 10 rather than 5 parts symptomizes this both here and in the 2 following symphonies.

The first movement begins with a 45-bar introduction that is to have an important influence on the work as a whole. A greater contrast to the explosive opening of *The Gothic* could scarcely be imagined. A bare-fifth chord of E, softly held by the 3 timpanists, is reinforced by low woodwind. Against this brooding stillness, pizzicato cellos and basses pick out an uneasily chromatic theme.

Ex 1 'Cellos, basses pizz.

Within its first 4 bars Ex. 1 includes all 12 notes of the chromatic scale – indicative of the tonal ambiguity that informs much of the music. Many of the symphony's themes display similar tendencies, and those that are more plainly diatonic are frequently contradicted by the textures in which they appear. There are places in this work

[1] The finale only requires 8 horns, and at a pinch this number might suffice for the scherzo, though that would put a great strain on the players and lose the advantages of a spatial disposition of forces.

where Brian approaches the frontiers of 'atonality'. Ex. 1, however, is no approximation of a tone-row, though it does possess
important motivic functions, especially through figure *x* and the
tritone interval which it spans.

The introduction moves towards a climax in three great waves
of sound, each time gaining in volume and weight of texture.
Twice more Ex. 1 appears in the bass, imparting the suggestion
of a passacaglia to the music. At the summit of the third and
biggest 'wave' (with Ex. 1 sounding on all bass instruments) the
main body of the movement crashes in, *Allegro Assai*.

After *The Gothic*, it is perhaps surprising to discover that what
ensues is a concise sonata-form – indeed a more orthodox example
than *The Gothic*'s first movement, economical in its material and
only modifying the conventional design so far as to include references to the introduction. Brian thus produces a much more
unified structure for the first part of his symphonic scheme: a
unity to which the material itself, varied but concentrated and in
no danger of over-expansion, is well fitted.

The first subject-group consists of 3 themes, the first and third
of which (Exx. 2 and 3) are restless, energetic, and closely related
(Ex. 3 – typically presented in canon – appears to grow out of an
inversion of the bass line of Ex. 2). They frame a brief, *dolce*
second theme, entrusted mainly to solo woodwind. All 3 make
prominent use of the falling tritone.

Brass chords modulate towards E major, and after a pause the
second subject, *Più Lento e Semplice*, begins in that key. Again
there are 3 themes, chiefly entrusted to the strings and all fairly
diatonic in nature, as the first (Ex. 4) shows: but they are presented
with highly complex accompanying patterns for horns, harps,
woodwind and *divisi* strings, blurring their apparent simplicity.

From rich and heady melodies the music suddenly changes to a
sparse simplicity: a mysterious codetta where solo brass, woodwind, celesta and harp play tranquil descending phrases in which
the shape of *x* may be clearly discerned. Then a whispering
passage of rapidly-accumulating semiquaver string figuration
leads directly into the development section.

This is notably brief, and begins with a vigorous discussion of
Ex. 2 which is quickly brought to an *fff* climax. Suddenly, however, it breaks off to reveal, as if in the middle distance, a totally
different sound-world in the shape of a weird central episode.
Flutes, glockenspiel and first harp play Ex. 1, the theme of the
introduction, in ghostly augmentation against a passionate,
chromatically-descending viola line, while lower woodwind,
second harp and pizzicato strings accompany with an ever-
changing pattern of interweaving arpeggios and strangely-
inflected scales. There is something dream-line in the effect: it
suggests that, despite the main movement's foreground activity,
the enigmatic music of the introduction is still going on in the
background, and has yet to be reckoned with.

The strange mirage dissolves back into the development, which
is now discovered exploring the second subject group. Ex. 4 is
heard simply and lyrically on a solo cello in C major, accompanied
by solo violin and viola; then *sonore*, in E major, on all cellos and
basses. The tempo quickens, and a distorted version of the second
subject's second theme on bassoons and cellos, punctuated by
excited off-beat woodwind chords, leads straight into the recapitulation. All six themes from the exposition are re-introduced
in the same order, though with considerable further development
and complete re-scoring. However, at the point where formerly

the codetta had begun, there is now a massive outburst for full
orchestra:

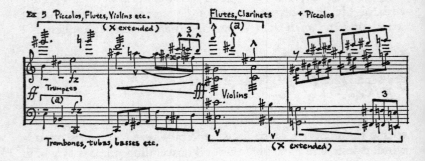

Several thematic elements are combined here, but the most
important is the extension of figure *x*, whose appearance at what
is in fact the climax of the movement begins to suggest that it has
the function of a 'motto'. The music now subsides into a bare
coda, with no further thematic reference, until softly marching
timpani introduce a variant of 5*a*, sinisterly descending on trombones and tubas, and the drummers close the movement with a
soft reiteration of their opening chord.

This spare, lean movement has something of the character of a
prelude – an impression enhanced by the fact that it seldom leaves
the key of E or its near neighbours. In the overall scheme of the
symphony, it functions as a 'curtain-raiser' to the main action. In
contrast to its clear-cut sonata structure, the slow movement,
which follows without a break, conforms to no traditional pattern.
Instead, the influence of *The Gothic*'s more open forms makes
itself felt for the first time. On closer study this movement – the
biggest in the symphony – resolves into three great spans of
music, all part of a single flow, yet thematically almost completely
independent, each echoing characteristics of the others with no
exact correspondences, and maintaining very impressively a
general elegiac mood. The variety and brilliance of the scoring, by
turns stark, subdued, shimmering and incandescent, is astonishing.

The movement begins at the simplest possible textural level,
with a poignant theme for unaccompanied cor anglais.

Taken over, *doloroso*, by first oboe, it is clothed in rich, dark harmony by woodwind, violas and cellos. Despite the appearance of other material, Ex. 6 is the main theme of the movement's opening span, though Brian subjects it to a typically free development by which its intervallic content is frequently altered, only its rhythms, especially that of figure *6a*, remaining constant. Before development has proceeded far, however, there is an interruption: 2 bars of dead-march rhythm for stopped horns and 2 sets of timpani. At this point such an incursion is hardly explicable, but it feels like an omen – a portent whose fulfilment we shall recognise in the funeral march of the symphony's finale.

Development resumes in contrastingly scintillant orchestration, with imitative entries of *6a* as a canon at the tritone, and passes to a new variation of Ex. 6 as a sweeping cello tune marked *Suave*. Eventually a stark outburst (for full strings, timpani and 4 bassoons) is reached, in which the main theme's components are hammered out between treble and bass with rhythmic dislocation and violent octave displacement:

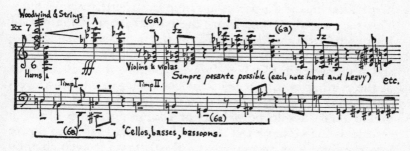

The passage is extended until it reaches a *fff* climax; and without

a break the second span of the movement begins with a new woodwind theme, presented over an ostinato in harp and timpani. The theme extends into a horn solo and an intensely lyrical passage for strings alone, marked *affetuoso*. Then Ex. 8 returns in a new, warm orchestral colouring, as part of a richly contrapuntal development. Among the accompanying figures something not wholly unlike Ex. 6 may be discerned – for here, as in *The Gothic*, Brian is able to use *similar* themes to suggest relationships without exact parallels. Throughout this movement, in fact, he continues to hint at the influence of Ex. 6, though he never reintroduces the theme itself.

As in the first span, the main material is developed until the arrival of a harsh, angular passage: this time, however, the outburst is not a further development but a new episode, around which the second span centres in a suggestion of ternary form. Beneath heroic triadic figures in horns, trumpets and strings, a stiff, jagged theme arises on bassoons, trombones, tubas, cellos and basses, and stalks along, assisted by timpani and unpitched percussion. It affords a clear stylistic parallel with Ex. 7 although its notes relate neither to Ex. 7 nor Ex. 8; and like Ex. 7 it rises to a stark climax, with the brass much to the fore.

Abruptly there is a complete change of texture: Ex. 8 returns on clarinets against a glittering background of celesta chords, harp glissandi, and a 4-part susurration from flutter-tongue flutes. This section, while completing the ternary form of the second span with further working of Ex. 8, also serves as a transition – referring back to the first span with another theme similar to Ex. 6 and at the same time looking forward, hinting at the main theme of the third span. Brian maintains continuity chiefly with ever-shimmering textures. These continue in celesta and tremolo violins while a solo horn hints at Ex. 6; then harp glissandi resume as the violins state a 3-note figure that is soon to flower into the third-span theme (Ex. 9 below). Brian is even able, by maintaining onward movement with a horn-and-timpani ostinato, and textural interest with harp and celesta chords and swirling demisemiquavers in divided strings, to insert an entirely new episode whose chief material – a canonic figure on flutes, oboes, and cor anglais – appears nowhere else. But at length the glitter fades and, with jagged downward-thrusting figures on trumpets and tubas, the final span of the movement begins.

A trilling violin solo leads swiftly to a passionate outburst in which the main theme is declaimed in an orchestral tutti.

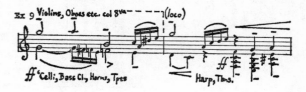

The solo violin returns to elaborate Ex. 9 in heroic octave double-stopping against shifting chromatic harmonies in horn and cor anglais. A forceful orchestral development of the downward-thrusting brass figure ensues before rising phrases for woodwind alone lead to the movement's extraordinary climax. This is a passage for full orchestra marked *Passionato mais sempre mesto*, which combines the third-span material with the shimmering textures of the second. Bassoons, tubas, cellos and basses take up Ex. 9 and extend it into a long, expressive melody; clarinets, horns and trumpets recall the brass figure and suggest more parallels with Ex. 6, while the whole is enveloped in a blizzard of glittering scales on flutes, oboes, harps, violins, and violas, changing soon to flutter-tonguing woodwind, tremolo violas and harp glissandi. After this the textures thin out, ushering in a bare coda in which fragments of the main theme are heard. A solo horn sings 9*a* over tremolo strings. Cellos and basses answer with 9*b*. The final cadence, for strings alone, is approached over a pedal F drum-roll, and ends the movement in a kind of harmonic shiver. Beginning as a superimposition of chords of B and E flat minor, it dissolves through multiple appogiaturas into E; and the very last note, G sharp, confirms the key as E Major.

Now comes the so-called 'battle' scherzo: but no extra-musical associations can explain this staggering torrent of orchestral invention. It is one tremendous individible musical organism, conceived in one pounding, unyieldingly fast tempo, built out of a single theme and a multitude of ostinato patterns. Ex. 10 gives a selection of these ostinati from different parts of the movement, and it can be seen that most adhere to the simplest tonic-dominant formulae. The material of the scherzo is in fact the most diatonic in the symphony, as befits a movement dominated by the char-acteristic sounds of the French horn. Nevertheless, Brian main-

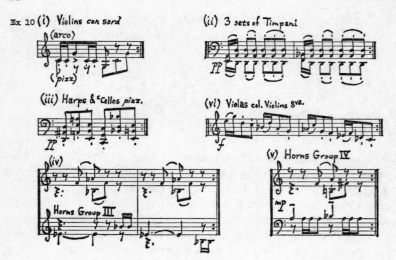

tains tonal ambiguity by a method already suggested in the slow movement's final cadence: bitonality. Straightforward the material may be, but much of it appears in 2 keys at once, causing a tension and violent tonal conflict that is not easily resolved.

The opening, quiet and magical, foreshadows the struggle in an evocative combination of C and D. Repeated notes on 2 harps build up a chord on D, against which we hear a flickering C-G tonic-dominant pattern (Ex. 10*i*) on violins and violas. For the first time in the symphony a piano is heard, with light, dancing chords; then a second piano joins in, and all 3 sets of timpani pound out a new ostinato figure (Ex. 10*ii*), apparently confirming D (minor) as the main key. Over this, in the clearest C major, enter the first group of 4 horns.

Ex.11 is the movement's only real theme, and it is almost exclusively the property of the first horn-group. When Group II enter (over a new ostinato (Ex. 10*iii*) in harps and pizzicato strings); Group III (over another in bassoons and timpani); and Group IV (over a spiccato development of 10*i* in full strings), it is soon apparent that they are only allowed to play yet more ostinati. (Ex. 10*iv* and *v* are examples.) As if to confirm their pre-eminence, Group I return with Ex. 11 in canon, still in C, over their accompanying piano-and-timpani ostinato in D minor. The piano parts have become more virtuosic, but Brian was to do greater things for these additions to his orchestral forces in his next symphony.

So far all the activity has been fairly quiet, but now the music moves towards its first climax: a violent clash between C and D sharp, all 16 horns combining in a new whooping ostinato against 10*iii* in bassoons and strings. Repeated 6 times, this key-clash brings the first true fortissimo in the movement. From now on the entire orchestra is gradually brought into play, in a welter of rhythmic invention, but the interest remains centred on the vast concertante body of 16 horns, 2 pianos, and 3 sets of timpani. The pace never flags: the movement sweeps inexorably towards its culmination as the textures grow more complex, ostinato is piled on ostinato, and the rhythms take on an insistent, hypnotic quality that proclaims kinship with the great ostinato build-up of the third movement of *The Gothic*. As tension mounts the horn-writing becomes wilder and ever more taxing, gravitating into remote keys and providing plenty of opportunities for stereo antiphonal effects.

When yet another ostinato (Ex.10*vi*) appears on the scene the music seems to be gyrating giddily in a wild Dionysiac frenzy. As this point the organ makes its first appearance in the score, reinforcing the bass with a fiendishly difficult development of 10*vi* for pedals alone; and amid the furious activity Ex.11 returns, shared for once between Groups I and II of horns in a heroic canon, rock-like in C Major, while all around the rest of the orchestra swings from key to key with weird effect. Yet at length all instruments seem to agree on C major for a final drive to the climax. The unanimity is short-lived. The next 20 bars metamorphose previous ostinati in a crescendo of frightening intensity; and the climax, when it comes, is simple yet shattering. Four times the organ, trumpets, trombones and tuba blazon forth superimposed chords of B flat minor and D flat, each time contradicted by a whiplash-like D major from pianos, harps, woodwind and strings; until the music, relaxing at last, subsides via E flat towards C.

Ex. 11 is heard for the last time, on solo horn, over a C-G harp ostinato; and for the only time in the movement its last note is not C, but D. Yet even now there is no resolution: the harp continues its ostinato in C, while the accompanying harmony on violas and cellos suggests F minor. The end is a soft but dissonant final chord, almost a cluster, which mockingly combines elements of at least 4 keys. Woodwind spell it out, note by note, from the top downwards; violins flicker momentarily against it with Ex. 10*i*, and the movement vanishes. Abruptly, the finale breaks in.

If the scherzo is the symphony's single most brilliant invention, the finale contains its greatest and most deeply-felt music. It is a huge funeral march, less granitic but more wide-ranging than that in *The Gothic*, its character varying from passionate grief to elegiac lyricism. It does not reconcile the conflicts of the preceding movements: rather it intensifies and thus somehow ennobles them, and by its close connection with the first movement brings to fulfilment much which was only latent there. It is deeply tragic, and ends in the E minor darkness which *The Gothic* so narrowly avoided. But like all true tragedy its effect is cathartic and so, finally, inspiring.

Formally it is the freest and most subtle in design of the four movements, though it has something of the character of a slow rondo. The main 'Rondo subject', announced at the outset, comprises 3 distinct ideas:

The terse, ejaculatory string figure 12*a* is to appear many times, both as a punctuation-mark and heightener of tension. The melancholy clarinet melody 12*b*, which is presented over harp and pizzicato bass chords, not only begins with the extension of the symphony's opening figure *x* from Ex. 5, but on inspection proves to be closely derived from the first 5 bars of Ex. 1. It is to return in full only twice, but its opening figure makes additional appearances in an unexpected context. Its final phrase turns the falling tritone into a kind of anti-cadence, only resolved by the solo horn fanfare 12*c*, which is to prove ubiquitous as a rhythmic influence, pervading much of the movement.

The initial presentation of the Ex. 12 material leads to a shortened and otherwise varied restatement, with 12*c* reinforced by side-drum, bass drum and cymbals. Then a noble tune arises from brass and timpani; but this leads to wrathful interjections of 12*a*, now coupled with a reiterated figure of 2 fortissimo semi-quavers that strongly recalls 'Siegfried's Funeral March' from *Götterdämmerung*. The oppressive, grief-stricken atmosphere heightens, and suddenly a huge orchestral tutti bursts in, *Grandioso* – none other than the whole of Ex. 5 from the first movement (thus referring also to the opening of 12*b*) with the intervals of figure 5*a* inverted so that it becomes a tragic, aspiring motif. Brass, organ, percussion, piccolos, basses and low woodwind provide this apocalyptic interruption while strings and upper woodwind sound frenetically in high semitone oscillations.

There is a brief pause, and then a quiet episode brings tempor-ary relief, beginning with a new melody (distantly related to 12*b*) on oboes and cellos.

It continues more darkly with the ghostly horn fanfare 12*c* in F minor, over a soft timpani ostinato and tolling strokes on gong and deep bell. There is a swift crescendo, climaxing in a low growling E flat for timpani and basses, after which the angry slitherings of 12*a* bring a pale return of the 12*b* melody on flutes and violins. Then the first horn leads the way with 12*c* into the finale's central episode.

Here, for a space, there is a kind of peace, and the turbulent passions of the symphony are a little assuaged in music of elegiac beauty. It begins on cellos and basses alone, divided in 7 parts. The episode develops in a wonderful passage of austere yet tender melody – the opening bars well illustrate the grave beauty of the writing:

Soon the violas enter, adding another 3 parts to the texture; and then full strings, *con passione*, initiate a sweeping orchestral crescendo at whose summit another forbidding 4-bar tutti, this time combining Ex. 5 and 12*a*, brings darkness again.

Henceforth the music steers towards the ultimate climax in a series of three crescendi, all rising to fulfilment in the same inexorable dead-march tempo. The first, beginning on woodwind and strings accompanied by piano chords, reaches its summit in a *fff* tutti including organ, harp glissandi, and ferocious tremolos from both pianos, dying away with heavy trudging bass figures on trombones, tubas, and percussion. The second develops out of the first, with reiterated statements of the fanfare-figure 12*c* in diminution on horns and trumpets, rising from *pp* to *ff* over a timpani ostinato. The third and last, beginning *molto espressivo* in the strings, builds up rapidly until the 'Götterdämmerung' figure is being hammered out in C sharp minor by full orchestra (including organ and percussion) with a fierce tremolo in violins, violas and both pianos, supported by 8 horns. Tension is at fever-pitch until Ex. 5, again furnished with screaming high strings and woodwind, explodes upon the scene, crowning the finale in a last outpouring of bitter majesty, its effect made even more shattering through the addition of huge gong-crashes.

There is a pause while the echoes die away, and then follows a bleak, exhausted coda, with the character of a lament and a final *Grablegung*. Ex. 13 returns, frail and wistful, on solo viola and cello; then the sepulchral 12*c* with the tolling bell, leading to a final statement of the main theme on solo clarinet, and its falling-tritone descent on flute and oboe, which bassoons and cellos quietly turn into a perfect fifth. 12a grumbles away in the bass; timpani and bassoons softly recall the *Götterdämmerung* figure; and clarinet and bass clarinet cadence unwillingly but finally into the enveloping gloom of E minor. The last sound is the bare-fifth drum-roll, on 3 timpani, with which the symphony opened.

5 Symphony No. 3 in C sharp minor (1931–32)

1. *Andante moderato e sempre sostenuto e marcato*
2. *Lento sempre marc. e rubato*   3. *Allegro vivace*
4. *Lento Solenne*

The composition of a symphony, and its preparation in full score, are a fearful labour, involving intense emotional and intellectual activity and sheer physical effort. Yet a mere 6 days after completing Symphony No. 2, on April 12, 1931, Brian began sketching a further symphony, on an even larger scale. Incredibly, it seems likely that while engaged on the full score of No. 2 he was already pondering its massive successor.

A very large first movement was sketched by May 23, and the other movements followed in rapid succession, the finale being completed in draft on July 16. Work on the full score occupied most of the following year, and the entire work was finished on the evening of Saturday, May 28, 1932. At present it still, after 40 years, awaits a first performance.

In contrast to the composition of the Second Symphony, Brian in old age could recall little of the circumstances that surrounded the writing of No. 3, save that on completion the score was sent to Sir Henry Wood, who (probably due to the expense and immense difficulty) was unable to perform it.[1] But external details are hardly necessary. The music tells its own story: tells that the Second Symphony had been only the first ocean breaker in a great flood-tide of inspiration, now running at full height. Though written for a slightly smaller orchestra, Symphony No. 3 is in every other respect a bigger work than its predecessor – longer in duration, more adventurous in structure and texture, more tower-

[1] It may also have been seen by Edward Clark (Schoenberg's first English pupil, one of the staunchest British champions of modern music, who was then working for the BBC). Brian had a high regard for him, and it seems at this period Clark was interested in performing Brian's music.

ingly heroic in expression; and an even more striking individuality emerges very strongly from the whole tissue of the composition. If No. 2 spoke with the accents of tragedy, No. 3 is imbued
with a rock-like, elemental heroism, as of some great titan left
over from an earlier world. Nevertheless it is a somewhat enigmatic work: full of grandeur and high passion, yet slow to yield
up its inner meaning.[1]

The orchestra admits of an even greater variety of colour than
in No. 2. It comprises quadruple woodwind, plus E-flat clarinet
and double bassoon; 8 horns, 4 trumpets, 5 trombones (including
contra-bass), and 2 tubas; strings; 2 sets of timpani, organ, 2
pianos, 2 harps, xylophone, glockenspiel, celesta, bass drum, side-
drum, tenor drum, cymbals, gong, triangle, tambourine and
castanets. The organ is only an *ad libitum* extra, adding weight to
the final bars; but the role of the 2 pianos, compared to the
previous symphony, is enormously extended.

The score teems with new and exotic sounds: the textural
variety of the slow movement of No. 2 is here carried to much
greater lengths. The first 2 movements, especially, are a riot of
proliferating – almost exfoliating – tone-colours, many of them
astonishingly advanced for their time, achieved through an
extreme subdivision of the orchestra and by pushing each player's
individual technique to the limit. Yet a consistently adventurous
approach to sonority is merely one aspect of the symphony's
overall character, as a bold extension of musical experience in
terms of overriding technical and imaginative mastery. It is the
music of a creative mind at full stretch.

This is particularly apparent in the first movement – a vast and
weighty structure, which with the almost as massive second forms
the bulk of the whole work. The first movement of Symphony
No. 2 was essentially an orthodox, concise, sonata-form. That of
No. 3, while still retaining a sonata basis, is an enormous, labyrinthine expansion of the form, gradually unfolding with continually surprising modifications, the most important of which
stem directly from the richly imaginative orchestral textures, in
which the 2 pianos play such a leading part. They become foci of
attention, attaining a kind of independent, concertante role

---

[1] One possibly significant detail is that on the title-page, half-erased but plainly
readable, stands the boldly-pencilled word ALTARUS – presumably a title the
composer abandoned. The present writer is unable to trace its source.

that increases until the movement's natural culmination in a powerful cadenza for pianos and timpani. Thus if the first movement of Symphony No. 2 was something of a prelude, that of No. 3 is a drama in itself: the drama residing in its richness of form, material, textures and contrasts, rather than its use of tonality. As in the first movement of No. 2, the music seldom departs from the region of the tonic key for long. But whereas in No. 2 it was precisely the lack of tonal movement that produced the 'preludial' character by arousing expectation, here the insistently-stressed C sharp minor is a source of structural unity, the one hard, sure fact among a host of ever-changing ideas.

The Third Symphony begins with a strong, deliberate forward motion, full of a sense of heroic purpose.

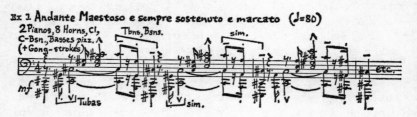

This brazen, striding introduction, tonally rooted to the spot in C sharp minor, opens with typically bold orchestration and introduces tough dotted rhythms, which are an almost obsessive characteristic of the work. With unvarying pace they spread through the whole orchestra, like the tramp and murmur of a great army; reach a massive climax; and subside, still in C sharp minor, to make way for the first subject (Ex. 2). The tune could be described as ballad-like, were it not for the harmonic complexity of the accompaniment. The melody appears on solo clarinet and strings divided in up to 10 parts, and the abrupt change of texture is another of the work's typical features.

No sooner has Ex. 2 been heard than there is a further change: a kind of linking episode in which the 1st Piano emerges with an arabesque-like variation of the tune, supported by solo wind instruments. The episode brings a return of Ex. 2, sonorous on horns, clarinets, bassoon and piano II, against a vigorous counterpoint in piano I and strings. Having restated the first subject, the music plunges into a powerful transition passage. 4 horns, their

Ex 2 Più Lento e espress
Solo Cl. & Strings.

rhythm supported by side-drum, hold a steadfast, pulsing C-sharp; violins, violas, cellos and piano I swirl in repeated demi-semiquaver flourishes; piano II and brass add their voices in heavy chords; while in extreme bass and treble a new, angular, dotted-rhythm theme pursues its course in gawky imitation between basses, tubas, and bassoons, and flutes, oboes, and xylophone. A typical Brian contrapuntal complex, in fact, reminiscent of no other composer. One of its functions is to make the first decisive move outside the main key, towards the second subject, which begins, on strings alone, in B minor.

After the energetic *Allegro moderato* of the transition, the extensive second subject unfolds at a more leisurely pace. It passes from strings, to woodwind, horns, and pianos, to full orchestra, and contains several distinct ideas. Ex. 3 gives the first and last of these in order of appearance.

Ex. 3*b* subsides onto a low pedal D, over which there suddenly appears one of the most astonishing masses of orchestral sound in modern music.

It is a teeming, fantastic, multitudinous noise. Soft gong-strokes maintain the beat. 2 cors anglais slowly descend in major thirds. Clarinets, bass clarinets and bassoons play fluttering, bubbling tremolos and scale figures. A celesta sounds ghostly chords. Piano I plays solo, with floating, disembodied arpeggios. Piano II and side-drum keep up a pulse of muttering demisemiquavers. And the strings, divided in no less than 20 parts, rustle with an insect-like activity of repeated demisemiquavers, muted and unmuted, *col legno* and *ordinario*, arco and pizzicato, in dynamics varying from *pp* to *ff*, and superimposing, within each quaver beat, groups of 3 notes against 4 against 5 against 6 against $7\frac{1}{2}$. The multi-overlapping rhythms, interlocking dynamics, radical subdivision of the orchestra and variety of attack are wholly unprecedented. Looking at these pages, one is reminded of nothing so much as the opening bars of the original (1952) version of Karlheinz Stockhausen's orchestral piece *Punkte*.

The amazing sound subsides as suddenly as it arose, and it does not return. (None of Brian's habits is so disconcerting, and disarming, as his 'throwaway' use of textural procedures that might occupy a fashionable *avant-garde* composer for life.) Piano I continues to spin wraith-like arpeggios against ponderous dotted-rhythm chords from trombones and tuba. The tension increases; both pianos join in a repeated rhetorical flourish against gong-crashes; and so introduce an impassioned restatement of the whole second subject. The whole passage has in fact been another transition of the kind with which Brian is enlarging the structure of the movement.

Ex. 3 and its fellows now return in the tonic C sharp minor, in very full orchestration, with skirling flutes and piccolos, uneasy, chromatically-shifting trumpet figures, and virtuosic concertante writing in both pianos. The restatement, reaching a huge climax, is broken off by a passage which acts as both transition and codetta. Beginning urgently on pizzicato lower strings and pianos, it returns the music to the tonic yet again, and accelerates until, with pounding C-sharp chords, the development breaks out *Allegro con brio*.

Perhaps 'development' is an inadequate term, for what we now hear is new material. In *The Gothic* we saw Brian modifying the structure of a sonata-form first movement towards its end; here we are faced with a more radical re-thinking of the design. It is the first of many wholly original symphonic movements in which Brian produces a very free, unpredictable chain of events against the implied background of sonata form. Here he has composed a central section which begins as an episode and gradually assumes the function of a development, approaching the exposition material, as it were, from the outside. The reasons for such modification are clear. Brian is writing an exceptionally broad-paced movement in the course of whose exposition both main subjects have already been heard twice. What he requires now is contrast of pace, mood, and material.

Accordingly the central section begins in the fastest tempo so far with a new theme in woodwind and strings and recurrences of the pounding chords, though the prevailing dotted rhythms in the accompanying figures ensures a certain continuity. After a time the tempo slows for a second new theme – a broad, noble A-flat melody marked *sempre dolente* and played sonorously *sul G* by violins, with an accompanying bass figure that bears a strong resemblance to the main theme (6b) of *The Gothic*'s third movement. Heavy brass take over the figure, and it is worked up, with the violin theme, into a magnificent contrapuntal complex. Yet again C sharp exerts an irresistible attraction, and into that key the music cadences. Since the close of the exposition the pianos have been silent; now they burst on the scene with a new idea (Ex. 4).

The pianos' massive ascending chords (4a) are clearly derived from the symphony's opening bars (Ex. 1), and this reference to the material of the introduction shows that the music is moving towards real development. The terse accompanying figure 4b, though, is certainly new – one of those simple, basic motives which Brian can use to generate enormous developmental processes. It is to prove particularly fruitful throughout the rest of the movement.

The re-entry of the solistic pianos leads to true development at

last: figure 2a reappears on strings and muted brass, and then the music plunges abruptly and dramatically into E flat minor for a stormy re-working of the whole first subject. The strings are reinforced in this by xylophone, glockenspiel and brass, accompanied by the pianos with brilliant semiquaver passage work (actually a highly virtuosic canon between the two instruments). The pace increases with a development of 4b on woodwind against pizzicato strings and xylophone, while the pianos dominate with a stream of hammering chords. Trumpets and tubas join the fray, the repetitions of 4b become more insistent, and at the peak of the excitement a brusque bare-fifth chord of C sharp announces the recapitulation.

The tempo eases (*Meno Allegro*) and Ex. 2 is grandly recalled, in canon with itself, on strings, woodwind and tubas, with gong-crashes and pealing bell-like scales from horns and trumpets. However, it soon quietens, with elegiac string writing, in the direction of D minor. As in the exposition, there now follows a linking passage. But not the *same* passage: again the pianos are brought to the fore with semiquaver arabesques, but apart from references to Ex. 2 in muted violins, the main substance is 4b, heard first on 2 sets of timpani, then on violas and cellos.

In due time the transition brings a return of the second subject. All its elements are recalled, mainly by brass and woodwind, against a bravura thunder of octaves in contrary motion from the pianos; later woodwind and strings join in a further, B minor development of 3*a*. Finally 3*b*, also, returns, and rises to a mountainous climax on full orchestra. That subsides; but a mysterious ostinato on basses and bassoons causes a sudden, expectant blaze-up on the dominant of C sharp. And both pianos, the stage finally their own, crash in *Allegro Maestoso* with what, to all intents and purposes, is a cadenza.

The cadenza is unaccompanied, except for the 2 timpanists. (Was this combination suggested to Brian by the strange piano-and-timpani cadenza that Beethoven wrote for the piano arrangement of his Violin Concerto ?). It is built strictly out of Ex. 4 – the pianos elaborating on 4*a* in booming chords, the timpani punctuating their statements with pounding developments of 4*b*. Eventually the pianos conclude on a decisive C sharp minor triad, the drums beat a rapid tattoo, and the orchestra launches into the coda – which, standing outside the main body of the movement, balances up with the introduction by drawing all its material from there. Thus it sticks firmly to the home key, and transforms material from Ex. 1, dominated by ferocious dotted rhythms and the beat of a tenor drum. The music, marked 'heavy as possible to the close', rises to a last great outburst on full orchestra, including pianos, and the movement ends in a dogged C sharp minor with the same sense of titanic inevitability with which it began.

The slow movement, in E minor, is almost as large, like a looming mountain range at the symphony's centre. It combines a stormy grandeur with moments of great tenderness and simplicity. Its complicated structure develops at least 4 principal themes with additional episodes. After the brazen splendours of the first movement, it begins (Ex. 5) tentatively, creeping in with no clearly-

defined theme. At first there is merely a soft drum-beat, a slippery, changeable 5-note figure (*x*) in the cellos, and alternating chords in clarinets, basses and bassoons. (Ex. 5*a*, the first bar, gives the essentials). Over that background a solo violin makes a brief, rhapsodic entrance (Ex. 5*b*). Its decorative trills and grace-notes give no hint of a true theme; yet, as in 5*a*, there are certain motivic shapes here that are to prove important.

Then the orchestra breaks into passionate utterance:

These 2 bars are only the beginning of a huge sweep of music – but they are the constant element, which, undergoing radical variations at each subsequent appearance, nevertheless constitute the movement's main theme. Note that the theme itself is a combination of several small-scale motives, each capable of separate development: after the broader lines of the first movement the tendency seems now to be towards a multiplicity of tight, self-contained units.

The big tutti thus unleashed ascends to the movement's first climax: a variation of Ex. 6 against furious woodwind tremolos and harp glissandi. (The harps, which made little contribution to the first movement, now become an important element in the texture, whereas the pianos recede into a subordinate role.) This climax, incidentally, is one of the rare occasions on which Brian uses the Elgarian marking *nobilmente*. It dies away, through horn-calls and rippling arpeggios from solo flute and clarinet, to a longer-breathed, expressive theme, announced by violins, oboes, and horns:

(Note the development of figure *x* from Ex. 5*a*, used as a counter-point.) The textures here are still quite complicated; but Ex. 7 makes a transition to an idea of complete simplicity, first heard on solo flute, and then passing to solo violin:

At this point all the principal material of the movement has been introduced, and there now ensures an impressive episode whose main thematic idea seems derived from figure *y* in Ex. 5*b*. Beginning with austere chords for woodwind, harps and strings, it grows swiftly into one of the craggy, looming masses of orchestral sound that are so typical of Brian's orchestral thinking, and tails away at length in a smoothed-out version of Ex. 5*b* for clarinets, horns, violins and violas.

A further variation of Ex. 6, quiet and adorned with cascading woodwind scales but still imbued with an enormous latent power, now burgeons into another huge orchestral paragraph. Almost imperceptibly Ex. 7 is drawn into combination with it, and then a brief calm episode, in which harps and 8 muted horns hold a soft dotted-rhythm ostinato on G, presages yet another variation of Ex. 6 in bolder colours, in C sharp minor. The terse 2-note bass figure of the original Ex. 6 is transformed into 3 tolling C-sharps on trumpets and timpani – a pattern that persists as the textures thin out and the solo violin returns in a flight of cadenza-like arabesques. Here, at the still centre of the movement, it dominates the scene, and the music hangs immobile in a tranced, melancholy beauty while the violin spins its stream of song against a soft woodwind background.

At length a gentle cadence into E prompts the return of Ex. 8, in varied form, shared as a canon between upper and lower strings. It is taken up by solo trumpet over trombone chords, and once more the air becomes charged with sterner emotions. Another daring passage of orchestral virtuosity, pitting 2 harps, 2 pianos, glockenspiel and xylophone against the flickerings of 4 piccolos, 4 muted trumpets, and pizzicato strings, leads with mounting excitement into the ultimate variation of Ex. 6, in E major. This

signals the re-emergence of the pianos into the limelight, with
glissandi and crashing chords, and they continue to play a
prominent part in the final towering climax which now arises, at
whose height may be discerned elements of all the movement's
principal themes. It culminates in a *risoluto* chordal outburst for
pianos and brass, referring back to that which succeeded the first
appearance of Ex. 8. In a quiet coda, all passion spent, a solo oboe
now mournfully plays a fragmentary recollection of that theme,
molto teneramente, semplice, mais mesto. The movement closes, sad
but clear-eyed, in E minor, with a cold, austere sound: a repeated
cadence for solo flute, floating like a sigh above quiet, echoing
chords from horn, trombones, and tubas.

The scherzo is the only movement that can be described simply
and succinctly. Unlike the wholly individual, continuously-
developing movements we have met in *The Gothic* and Symphony
No. 2, it is an orthodox ternary-form Scherzo and Trio. In this
respect, as also in emotional character and tonality (A major – a
key seldom touched elsewhere in the work), it seems to stand
outside the main symphonic current – basically providing an
interlude and effective contrast, with its strong, driving rhythms.
Also, for most of its length Brian employs an orchestra no larger
than Bruckner's. (The pianos are silent in this movement.)

The opening section has immense rhythmic impetus. It begins
with a pounding, fanfare-like idea announced by the trumpets.

This breezy theme generates an exciting and vigorous first section
with several subsidiary ideas such as a triplet motif for flutes and
pesante marching quavers in woodwind and strings, worked up
together to a brief climax, followed by modulations away from
the home A. At the double bar the time-signature changes to 6/8
and a contrastingly gentle theme is introduced in F, by the (for
Brian) unusually delicate combination of flute and string quartet.

The tune is developed, over an insistent pedal F in timpani, by flute, horn, and muted strings, after which a crisp fanfare of Ex. 9, in D, brings a return of the opening material. The recapitulation is foreshortened, and 3 bars for percussion alone lead to the Trio which again moves the music into the region of F. It has a double theme:

and the two disarmingly simple ideas are presented separately and together in a variety of orchestral guises. The section ends on a reiterated F from trumpets and timpani.

Brian now returns to the Scherzo material, bringing his full orchestra into play at last and restating everything in stronger, bolder colours. In fact he is not content merely to restate, but powerfully develops Ex. 9 and its subsidiaries with much additional brass and percussion. The key is again A, and in A also Ex. 10 returns, in very bright and joyful orchestration, decoratively adorned by harps and woodwind, and spurred on its way by the clacking of castanets. Then Ex. 9 intervenes for the last time, and the Scherzo concludes decisively with a stark fanfare of trumpets and trombones.

The finale returns us to the more highly-charged emotional world of the first 2 movements. Solemn, slow-moving, yet full of an intense lyricism and even, at times, a remote magic that is to become an ever stronger element in Brian's scores, it moves towards a conclusion of such elemental power that 'victory' seems an inadequate term to describe it.

Its opening (Ex. 12, opposite page), with the main theme on solo bass clarinet, may seem superficially to resemble that of the finale of Symphony No. 2. But the theme, its presentation, and the processes it engenders, are far different. Note the insistent G-sharp on the horns, against which the melody clashes. The key is ambiguous, more E than C sharp (the simultaneous suggestion of relative major and minor is very characteristic). But the stress on G-sharp gives that note the feeling of a dominant: the listener begins to anticipate that the key of C sharp is not only the immediate, but the ultimate goal of the symphony.

Gradually, out of the simple beginning, there flows a great current of slow, noble and eloquent polyphony, complete with Brian's typical canonic imitations, growing organically from the bass clarinet's first notes and full of multifarious motivic shapes which all have their function in later developments. Ex. 12 traces the mere beginning of this grand process through the movement's first 24 bars. Note the direction in German ('each instrument must *always* sing') – one of several to be found throughout the score. Their use was to be greatly extended in the following symphony.

The movement has the approximate shape (though not the detail) of a sonata-form, and the Ex. 12 complex and its continuation can be considered the first subject. Much the most important theme is 12*a*, which like its near-inversion 12*c* derives straight from the first bass clarinet phrase. The opening statement of the

first subject rises to the movement's first climax (marked by the re-entry of the 2 pianos) and then dies away, with a wriggling ostinato figure on oboe and strings, passing to solo piano and pizzicato cellos and basses.

Suddenly there is a moment of wonder. Muted strings hold down a quiet, densely-clustered chord on F-flat, and far away the clear tones of an off-stage trumpet sound a distant fanfare. The harmony shifts onto F-natural, and a solo horn, equally far in the distance, sounds an answering call. That is all: a sudden, totally unexpected romantic image, apparently unconnected with the rest of the symphony, yet having a heart-catching effect. Its magic is one of suggestion. Somewhere, we feel, far beyond this work's horizon, events are stirring, battles are being joined, other worlds lie undiscovered. It is another of Brian's 'revelatory' moments, qualifying the foreground activity by showing a mystery behind them; and this particular evocative image of the distant fanfare will occur, always in different contexts, in other symphonies.

The fanfares lead in this case to an energetic resumption of 'foreground' activity: a strong passage of development marked *Stark und Dunkel*, based on 12a, for strings, lower woodwind, and brass. This, however, is itself only a transition to the movement's other main theme:

The flowing tune is introduced first by double basses, with only a sparse cello accompaniment. But from these slight textures Brian, by repetition, extension and development, begins to work towards a splendid climax. Ex. 13 is soon heard on solo oboe, with woodwind and horn counterpoints, against triplet figuration in the harps and splashes of colour from the celesta. It is taken up by full strings, by cor anglais and bass clarinets; and becomes itself a mere counterpoint as the pianos return to their concertante role, developing the harps' triplet figures and offshoots of Ex. 12 with great virtuosity. The grandeur increases; the triplets pass to full strings; the pianos respond with thunderous octave passages; and horns, trombones and tubas weigh in with a series of canonic entries of 12*a*, leading to a great outburst of orchestral power.

The briefest of pauses brings only a resumption of the struggle. Bassoons and cellos powerfully develop 12*a* against reiterated *forzato, con passione* semiquavers on the violins, blaring trumpets, and whooping horns, and the pianos storm in on a great swelling wave of semiquaver figuration derived from 12*d*, a figure which begins to acquire increasing importance. Then the tumult fades away on E, with 12*b* turned into a quiet ostinato by piano I.

At this point begins a recapitulation and extension of Ex. 12 (from the entry of 12*a*) in much fuller and grander orchestration, with 12*d* as a continual groundswell, rising and falling in pianos, bassoons and cellos. It builds up to a huge climax, attaining its summit in C but swiftly declining once more, into E, to another low quiet piano ostinato.

The 'second subject', Ex. 13, now returns in C sharp minor, but with the ubiquitous 12*d* as a counterpoint. In fact that little figure seems capable of endless sequential extension to power the large climaxes – and it now sets the ultimate one in motion. The music, its rise and fall like that of a mighty sea, moves through D to E major; the full brass enter, the pianos rumble on, strings and woodwind passionately carry Ex. 13 higher and higher; the organ, should one be available, also adds its voice. At the height of the great tide of sound, Brian forsakes his themes entirely, and concludes the work with four crushingly decisive bars which he labels 'Epilogue'. Here is no Baxian meditation, but a heavy, reiterated march-rhythm for full forces, with gong, full percussion, organ, and swirling glissandi for both pianos and harps. It pounds away at C sharp, thus fulfilling and balancing the G-sharps with which the movement began, and distantly echoing the introduction to the first movement. But it drives inexorably to C sharp *major*, and a last conquering chord that swells to a deafening *ffff*. Thus, with a brusquely triumphant explosion of dynamic energy, ends this massive, enigmatic and fascinating symphony.

6   'Das Siegeslied': Symphony No. 4 (1932–33)

1. *Maestoso*   2. *Lento*   3. *Allegro* (*Bewegt*)

Brian's prodigious creative energies showed no sign of flagging. On June 20, 1932, less than a month after completing the Third Symphony, he was making the first sketches for yet another large-scale work – his most monumental symphony since *The Gothic*. Though not quite as long as No. 3, the new piece reverted to the idea of an orchestra complete in every family of instruments; and again it was a vocal work – wholly so this time – requiring a large double chorus and solo soprano. Its text is Psalm 68 – 'Let God arise', and in choosing it Brian was returning to a subject he had essayed a quarter of a century before.[1] But, significantly, he now decided to set it in German, following Luther's version ('Es stehe Gott auf'); and he entitled the symphony *Das Siegeslied* – The Psalm of Victory.

Composition went ahead with Brian's customary speed. Pre-liminary sketching took until December 4, 1932, after which he made a final sketch in the form of a vocal score, the orchestra reduced to 3 staves. Throughout the rest of the following year Brian worked on the vast full score, which required 40-stave manuscript paper, completing it on December 10, 1933. The result is a monumental 3-movement work with a playing-time of some 43 minutes, scored for the following forces: solo soprano, double SATB chorus, 6 flutes (2 doubling piccolos and another alto flute), 2 oboes, 2 oboi d'amore, 2 cors anglais, bass oboe,

[1] The earliest known list of Brian's compositions, in *The Staffordshire Sentinel* of January 15, 1907, concludes with the entry 'Psalm, *Let God arise,* for chorus, soli, and orchestra, Op. 15'. No trace has ever been found of this work, and it was perhaps only sketched, since in the following year *The Vision of Cleopatra* was published with the same opus number.

E-flat clarinet, 4 B-flat clarinets, 2 bassett-horns, 2 bass clarinets, pedal clarinet, 4 bassoons, 2 double-bassoons, 8 horns, 4 trumpets, 5 trombones, 2 tubas, 2 sets of timpani, 2 harps, glockenspiel, xylophone, organ, celesta, gong, cymbals, bass drum, side-drum, tambourine, triangle, bell in C, and strings. Like its predecessors, the Fourth Symphony languished in obscurity for the next 30 years. The work is intimidating both in its difficulty and its uniquely sinister atmosphere, and its first performance, for a BBC broadcast in 1967, was far from satisfactory. At the time of writing, therefore, *Das Siegeslied* still awaits an adequate rendering.

It is in some ways the most disturbing of all Brian's works. Its general layout brings to mind the *Te Deum* of *The Gothic*: but whereas the *Te Deum* for the most part conveys a New Testament light and radiance, this baleful Psalm confronts us with the darkest of Old Testament passions. 'Psalm of Victory' leads one to expect something simply optimistic; but although the symphony begins in that vein, it traverses a great range of moods, few of which are simple – through the whole work, sometimes openly, sometimes beneath the surface, runs a current of brutal violence. The reader may be familar with the final chorus of Walton's *Belshazzar's Feast*, where the Jews exult over the fall of Babylon in the same pitiless, self-righteous tones as their late oppressors. A similar idea is the central expressive issue of *Das Siegeslied*, and Brian explores its implications in many ways. His magnificent brass writing here conjures up the sound of military bands, his march-rhythms the noise of the parade-ground, his choral writing the frenzied shouts of war hysteria. The huge *Gothic*-style orchestra is no longer used for range of timbres but for sheer *weight* of tone: the work abounds in deafening tutti passages. It is a shattering, armour-plated juggernaut of a symphony, and when, as in the slow movement, it penetrates more visionary regions, violence is only held in check, to burst forth nakedly at the climax. All told, *Das Siegeslied* occupies a position in Brian's *oeuvre* not dissimilar to that which Vaughan Williams's Fourth – written at the same period – does in his.

In fact, because of the explicitly Germanic content, it seems reasonable to note (as others have with Vaughan Williams) that Hitler came to power while Brian was engaged on this symphony. A keen student of German affairs, Brian was fully aware of the course events were taking, and *Das Siegeslied* certainly marks a

crucial – and painful – stage in his involvement with the German
tradition. Whether or not he intended a comment on Nazi
militarism, it is surely significant that his most violent work
should be so Germanic in spirit. There is, to begin with, Luther's
text of the warlike psalm: although Brian made an English singing
translation, it should never be used, for the voice-parts are
conceived wholly in terms of the harsh consonants and barking
vowels of German. That language must have seemed to Brian the
natural, the immediate contemporary medium through which to
portray the righteous zeal of the Psalmist. A further Lutheran
reference is the extraordinary use of *Ein' feste Burg* in the finale.
The score teems with German expression-marks and tempo-
indications. The symphony's grim, barbaric splendour brings to
mind the sinister glories of a Nuremberg rally.

Yet perhaps most astonishing is the *objectivity* that informs the
work. It is not the product of subjective violence within Brian,
but a deeply-imagined presentation of national violence, bare of
all illusions. It forces us to look the cruelty of war and the brutal-
isation of 'Victory' full in the face, and know them. When I hear
Brian described as a naïve man, I always think of this work. Only
a very sophisticated artist, with great clarity of vision, could have
conceived it.[1]

Structurally the symphony is Brian's freest yet. None of the
movements follows any conventional pattern, though there is the
suggestion – no more – of a ternary form in the first movement,
an even slighter suggestion in the slow movement, and a certain
amount of true recapitulation in the finale. The chorus is used
only in the outer movements, and the soprano only in the second.
Tonally the work is fluid: it is usually described as being 'in C',
but though it begins and ends in C major, the bulk of the sym-

[1] It suggests to me a strange parallel, which the reader may not find wholly
irrelevant. Superficially, no two composers could be less alike than Havergal Brian
and Adrian Leverkühn, the fictitious protagonist of Thomas Mann's great novel of
modern music and the corruption of Germany, *Doctor Faustus*; nor two works so
stylistically different than *Das Siegeslied* and Levrkühn's hellish oratorio, the
Apocalypsis cum Figuris. Yet both link in disturbing conjunction the Old Testament,
Lutheran Germany, and modern 'blood-boltered barbarism', and both intimate in
what I imagine as very similar ways in their 'urge to reveal in the language of music
the most hidden things, the beast in man as well as his sublimest stirrings'. It may
not be without significance that Mann made his composer-hero, like Brian, a
passionate admirer of Blake's verse, and that both Leverkühn and Brian – the one
in fiction, the other in reality – had written an anguished song-setting of *The
Defiled Sanctuary*.

phony takes place around other tonal centres, especially D and E: C simply provides the granite pillars on which the huge structure rests. At a more detailed level, it seems at first that musical events are largely dictated by the text. Closer inspection reveals much wide-ranging, symphonic development of 'family' groups of themes, similar to the *Te Deum* of *The Gothic* but on terser, more varied ideas. There are also thematic elements which recur in different movements, providing unity and also, on occasion, acting as 'leitmotives'. One of the most striking is an awesomely volcanic idea associated with the name of God – and its character leaves us in no doubt that He is a Jealous God in true Old Testament tradition:

The ensuing description of the symphony uses the text of Psalm 68 from the King James's Bible, with some minor alterations in accord with the sense of the version Brian set.

Das Siegeslied crashes into life in a blaze of pomp and splendour, with a thunderous C major march that has an almost Baroque magnificence:

Handel at his most grandiose might have penned a tune like that
(though without the parallel fifths), and the startled listener may
wonder if he is hearing a 20th-century symphony or the Sinfonia
to some outsize Coronation Anthem for a Hanoverian King. In
fact this opening is a masterly stroke. The heights of elation to
which the march soon climbs are a realisation in the grandest
terms of the conventional, superficial response to the triumphant
words of the Psalm. But Brian is concerned with the reality
behind the pomp, and soon the march dies away, with reiterations
of the rhythm 2a and a violin tremolo. Suddenly, the music steps
sheer into another world.

Enter the voices, quietly, with '*Es stehe Gott auf . . .*' ('*Let God
arise, let his enemies be scattered; let them also that hate him flee before
him*'). The tempo has not altered; the violin tremolo persists; the
key-centre has swung round to F. Seeming at first only a confused
mass of fearful voices, the choirs make their opening supplication
in a complex 8-part texture, through which *cuivré* horns shine
sinisterly forth. The violins' tremolo changes to a rustling
arpeggio, and as the texture thickens new shapes loom out on
horns and woodwind without attaining solid thematic status. The
music slows to 'very broad and massive', the choral texture
becomes tensely chromatic, and an awesome roll on the gong
seems momentarily to overwhelm the rest of the orchestra. Its
echoes die away to reveal a new *Allegro fuoco* tempo, propelled by
urgent repeated semiquavers on horns and trumpets.

'*Vertreibe sie wie der Rauch . . .*' ('*As the smoke is driven away, so
drive them away) as wax melteth before the fire, so let the wicked perish
at the presence of God*'). The choirs lead off with a vigorous, leaping
theme and an energetic semiquaver figure; they are soon accompanied by battering percussion and cascading figures in woodwind
and brass. The tension is rapidly whipped up to a massive cadence

into D, and a wild, tearing brass fanfare bursts its way hysterically through the orchestral fabric.

'*Die gerechten . . .*' ('*But let the righteous be glad; let them rejoice before God: yea, let them exceedingly rejoice*'). After the fanfare's last stark chord, Brian sets these words not with a melody, but to a frenzied *a capella* semiquaver ululation in rapidly-changing time-signatures. It starts on C but quickly reaches a very dark region of flat keys. Light, however, returns as the orchestra strikes in with a new march-tune in D major:

But this lasts little longer than the quotation, and a single *molto legato* woodwind bar leads straight into '*Singet Gott, lobsinget seinem Namen . . .*' ('*Sing unto God, sing praises to his name: extol him that rideth upon the heavens by his name JAH, and rejoice before him*'). The music here consists of increasingly fragmented and ever more violently-scored statements of the march-theme Ex. 3, passing through various tonalities and soon only recognisable through the prominence of the figure 3*a*, hammered out by brass and percussion. There is a vast climax at 'rejoice before him' which subsides into momentary calm in D minor. Horns, bassoons, timpani and harps quietly set a new scene in a *Più Lento e Semplice* tempo.

'*Der ein Vater ist der Waisen . . .*' ('*A father of the fatherless, and a judge of the widows, is God in his holy habitation. God setteth the lonely in families: he bringeth out those who are bound with chains: but the rebellious dwell in a dry land.*') Flutes and oboi d'amore lead off with a pastoral melody beneath which the first chorus gives an *espressivo* treatment to the opening words, suggesting a softening of the harsh emotional world we have experienced so far. Despite the grimness of his overall conception, Brian is fully responsive to the verses of the Psalm which enshrine more sympathetic human experience, and gives them all due weight. Indeed, it is precisely such tender episodes as this which emphasize the prevailing brutality. Soon an angry, downward-thrusting horn figure brings a fierce exultation to the setting of the last words. A toiling figure in the violins' low register urges the music onward, and as the

voices climb in a slow chromatic ascent, a development of this
figure is treated as a harsh, close canon in brass and strings:

Ex 4   CHOIRS I & II in 8ves.

ORCH.— All lines doubled at the lower 8ve

It rises to a huge D minor climax, with full voices and orchestra
enmeshed in close multiple entries of a further canon. The tension
increases, with a brutal excitement at the fate of the rebellious,
until, to a thrice-repeated cry of '*Gott!*', the apocalyptic Ex. 1
bursts in, on full orchestra.

'*Da du vor deinem Volk herzogen . . .*' ('*O God, when thou went forth
before thy people, when thou didst march through the wilderness; Selah:
The earth shook, the heavens also dropped at the presence of God: even
Sinai itself was moved at the presence of the God of Israel*'). As the
echoes die away a pair of horns give out a repeated G, indicating
a new key-centre. Chorus and strings begin *misterioso* in a triplet-
rhythm clearly derived from the bass of Ex. 1, but soon that awesome thunderbolt explodes again. Here Brian replaces the
Biblical '*Selah*' with another triple cry of '*Gott!*', leading straight
into a sinister 9/4 section, whose key is an uneasy C minor. The
earth shakes to furious trills on a battery of flutes, *cuivré* horns,
twistedly chromatic string figures, and an insistent, tolling C bell.
The tension mounts and the texture fills out over a furiously
active chromatically-rising bass, to a shattering climax which is
a third and most violent eruption of the 'Jealous God' motif Ex. 1,
reinforced by massive percussion and vicious lightning-flashes
from piccolos, flutes, E-flat clarinet and other woodwind. A huge
cadence is built up (for 'the God of Israel') by chorus, organ, and
full brass over an extension of the bass of Ex. 1, and culminates in
a gargantuan chord for the voices through which brass, organ
and drums swell out in an overwhelming crescendo that leaves
the hearer stunned. There is, very necessarily, a brief pause.

There has been quite as much sound and fury as the human ear can stand, and so the central section of the movement begins as soothing balm: a pastoral *Lento*, scored for the organ's sweetest mixture of gamba, dulcian and voix celeste; muted strings; a calm pizzicato cello figure; and tinkling harp arpeggios. Then solo bassett-horn and bass clarinet lead into an entirely *a capella* setting of the next words.

'*Du gabst, Gott, einem gnädigen Regen* . . .' ('*Thou, O God, did send a plentiful rain, whereby thou didst confirm thine inheritance when it was weary. Thy congregation hath dwelt therein: thou, O God, hast prepared of thy goodness for the poor*'). The sound of unaccompanied voices is a welcome relief to the listener's ear, but cruel demands are placed on the singers. The section opens simply and beautifully with an almost *da chiesa* air:

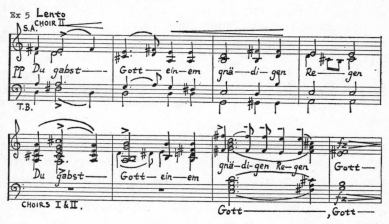

However, the textures soon become highly chromatic, unity being provided mainly by the presence of the figure *5a* in various forms. The part-writing is masterly, and the chromaticism is linear in origin, growing out of strict contrapuntal logic. The task of maintaining accurate pitch is, however, immense – far greater than (to name a roughly analogous instance) in the unaccompanied choral section of Delius's *Appalachia*. But diatonicism returns at the close, and the basses end the section gently with a perfectly straightforward cadence in B flat. There is a drum-roll on D, and the calm is shattered as the final section of the movement begins *Allegro vivo ma decisivo*.

'*Der Herr gab das Wort . . .*' ('*The Lord gave the word: great was the company of those that published it. Kings of armies did flee apace, and she that tarried at home divided the spoil*'). This is the cruellest music so far, and it conjures up a vision of pursuit and carnage after a great battle. It begins in a racing 4/4 with multiple canons on the first words in and between the choirs; but soon changes to an obsessive, galloping 6/8, sweeping through an orchestral landscape full of strange and malevolent sonorities. The vocal lines grow more chromatic again as the chorus takes upon itself the role of the fleeing Kings: they are hounded by bellowing tubas and wickedly flashing upper woodwind. Just as the 6/8 rhythm seems to have entirely taken control, a furious battering from the 2 sets of timpani slashes across it in 3/4. The music reels into 4/4 with terse trumpet and tuba figures snapping at the heels of the choruses' wailing semitones. The pursuit has become a rout, and horns and trumpets whoop in harsh triumph:

Ex 6

The end comes quickly after this, with a rallentando that halts the chase and a vastly inflated appoggiatura for full voices and orchestra that only grounds safely – in D – on the last beat of the final bar.

The slow movement, which follows after a short pause, contains some of the most imaginative music in Brian's entire output. Quite apart from its frightening climax, it has for much of its length a heady voluptuousness that is unparalleled in his work. Robert Simpson finds it 'Oriental' in character – and while there are no specifically exotic elements in the music, its strange atmosphere of mingled sensuousness and violence strongly supports the imaginative truth of that description. It adds a dreamlike, almost metaphysical dimension to the barbarism of the other movements.

It begins innocently enough, with another calm pastoral vision in D major. Harps and muted horns set up a tranquil lapping rhythm, with an important falling cello figure beneath it. Then a calm dialogue ensues between solo and alto flutes. The lapping rhythm returns, with a suave cello tune; then calm descending

scales on flute and harps; and finally a rapt and beautiful violin
solo which seems at first a direct link with the 'English pastoral'
tradition of such works as Vaughan Williams's *The Lark Ascending*. But this is no bird-song, rather a kind of passionate vocalise,
resounding in stillness, preparing the way for the soprano. It ends
on a high A harmonic, and the solo voice enters, *recit. a piacere*, in
a wholly unaccompanied bar.

'*Wenn ihr zwischen den Hürden . . .*' ('*Though you have lain among the
pots, yet shall ye be as the wings of a dove covered with silver, and her
feathers with yellow gold. When the Almighty scattered kings in it, it was
white as snow in Salmon*'). The lapping rhythm returns, in A major,
on full woodwind and harps, before the soloist launches out again
over a rich background of divided strings. Her original unaccompanied phrase was almost pentatonic, but the vocal line
now becomes intricately chromatic, moving phrase by phrase
among all the semitones within a limited compass. A more diatonic phrase, also heard at this point, provides much of the movement's main material through such developments as Ex. 7*a*:

For the silver wings of the dove, the voice is enveloped in a
glittering texture of solo violin, 4 flutes, 2 piccolos, glockenspiel,
celesta and 2 harps (playing alternately *normale* and in harmonics);
for the golden feathers the soprano duets with the solo violin. The
snow in Salmon brings development of Ex. 7 in augmentation on
the upper strings, against glowing sonorities for muted horns.

'*Ein Gebirge Gottes ist das Gebirge Basans . . .*' ('*The hill of God is
as the hill of Bashan; even an high hill as the hill of Bashan. Why leap ye,
ye high hills? This is the hill which God desireth to dwell in; yea, the
Lord will dwell in it for ever*'). Violins and violas, tremolo, sul
ponticello, hold a still, high octave G, while the soprano and
lower woodwind have a more expansive development of Ex. 7.
The high hills leap (or hop, as Brian's own translation has it) to a
quiet dotted-note figure which passes quickly among a number
of keys and sonorities – pizzicato cellos and basses, muted horns,
harps, and flutes and glockenspiel – over a bass drum roll. Ex. 7*a*

appears, and the music flowers in a lyrical expansion on much-divided strings. But suddenly there is a pause; and then the mood changes utterly.

'*Der Wagen Gottes . . .*' ('*The chariots of God are twenty thousand, even thousands of angels: the Lord is among them, in Sinai, in the holy place*'). The soloist delivers the words over harp glissandi, urgent flute tremolos, and a driving *Allegro Vivace* side-drum rhythm; while in the same rhythm, bassoons and muted trumpets go on the warpath. '*Heiligen Sinai*' is a thrilling chromatic descent from a top B for the soprano, and gives way to massive horn chords, the swelling roar of the gong, and a ferocious semiquaver rattling from xylophone, piccolos, oboes, and E-flat clarinet. There is another pause and the core of the movement – for orchestra alone – begins with a thunderous outburst for full orchestra, related to Ex. 1.

The echoes of this wrathful explosion die, only to be replaced by a purposeful *Allegro* beginning on strings alone. Here, perhaps, we have a graphic portrayal of those terrible angelic chariots. Over an insistent rhythm like a cosmic heartbeat, a long melody, smooth yet inexorable, unwinds sinuously on second violins and cellos. Gradually it is subsumed into the 'heartbeat' rhythm, as the music rises from key to key by semitonal steps. When the rhythm passes to 4 flutes and timpani it is heard against running pizzicato scales in lower strings and an eerie, minatory cross-rhythm in the trumpets:

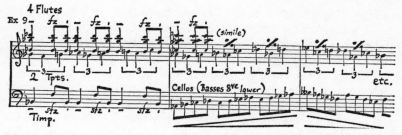

Soon the trumpets give tongue again with a cold, proclamatory figure derived from figure 8*a*. The beating rhythm swells to a mighty tumult, suddenly cut short to leave an E-flat timpani roll exposed; and then the climax comes with the blinding flash of Ex. 1, twice, in a version more apocalyptic than anything heard in the first movement – followed at once by a tremendous descent into the depths for organ and brass, as if the veil of heaven has been rent aside to reveal a black, bottomless abyss. It ends in a ponderous moan from trombones and tubas at the bottom of their register, as if the music is sinking out of sight. The whole passage has a quality of imagination that is Blakean in its intensity and Miltonic in its power. Indeed, this terrifying episode brings to mind the ruin of the fallen angels in *Paradise Lost*,

> pursued
> With terrors and with furies to the bounds
> And crystal wall of Heaven; which, opening wide,
> Rolled inward, and a spacious gap disclosed
> Into the wasteful Deep . . . . eternal wrath
> Burnt after them to the bottomless pit.

Yet perhaps even more terrible is the fact that the catastrophe is answered, after a pause, by music from on high that is tranquil and unmoved – by a weird orchestral texture, at once aloof and coldly voluptuous, created by solo flute, alto flute, bassett-horn and muted double basses, with feathery quaver figuration on celesta and 2 harps. The soprano re-enters, radiant, untroubled.

'*Du bist in die Höhe gefahren . . .*' ('*Thou hast ascended on high, thou hast led captivity captive: thou hast received gifts for men; yea, for the rebellious also, that the Lord God might dwell among them*'). The verse is sung twice: first with the solo voice floating through the texture, while the harp and celesta figuration is reinforced by the organ's gamba and dulcian stops, and transformations of Ex. 7 sound in divided strings. The second time the quaver figuration rises and falls in great waves on the strings, the woodwind texture thickens, and the organ adds its full weight to a climax with the soprano singing the last phrase as a passionate chromatic slide from a top B-flat. A stormy brass passage follows, leading to a thrice-repeated cadence into E major, punched home by trumpets, trombones and tubas and confirmed each time by broad, echoing chords on 6 horns. The movement dies away with a soft repetition of an E major triad in the lower brass.

The finale, the longest and most episodic of the movements, opens with a distinctly Brucknerian flavour. The E tonality of the slow movement's close is prolonged into the finale by a high sustained E tremolo in the violins, beneath which cellos and basses heave and the chorus state a kind of *Urthema*:

'*Gelobet sei der Herr täglich*' ('*Blessed be the Lord daily*'). The words are repeated in different shapes, with the chorus trying flatter keys, *cuivré* horns adding their sinister tones to the air of quiet expectancy, and the cellos trying to establish the key as C. The high E persists, however, until in the manner of things it assumes the feeling of a dominant. A cadential outburst cannot be long delayed, and suddenly, growing from a speck on the horizon to a blaze that fills the sky, A major is upon us (Ex. 11).

'*Gott legt uns eine Last auf . . .*' ('*who loadeth us with benefits, even the God of our salvation. And unto God the Lord belong the issues from death. But God shall wound the head of his enemies, and the hairy scalp of such an one as goeth on still in his trespasses*'). After the rhetorical pause at the end of Ex. 11, the music swings away in a loping 12/8

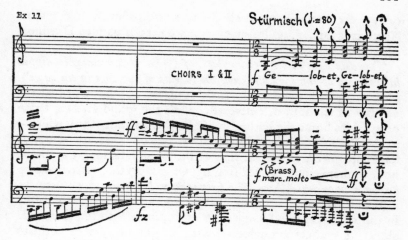

rhythm, with the air of a victory parade. The orchestration is blunter than in the preceding movement, with harsh, prominent brass. When the time-signature changes to 3/4, *Immer stürmisch und kräftig*, there is a definite flavour of military band music in the bold writing for horns and tubas. The pounding of marching feet is suggested by a steady crotchet beat maintained by both timpanists. In time, the music cadences into D major. The time changes to 6/4, and the mood to 'Solemn, broad and massive'. Full brass and organ pompously clear their throats; and choirs and orchestra launch into a grand world-bestriding tune:

'*Der Herr hat gesagt* . . .' ('*The Lord said, I will bring again from Bashan, I will bring my people again from the depths of the sea*'). It is a superb episode. Ex. 12 seems to unfold endlessly, in expansive contrast to the taut motivic working that has dominated the music so far. Decorated by joyful trumpet calls that generate a powerful quaver accompaniment, it climbs to a great climax in E major. There it is cut off, and a quiet cadence carries us into D minor, *Misterioso.*

'*Das dein Fuss in der Feinde blut . . .*' ('*That thy foot may be dipped in the blood of thine enemies, and the tongues of thy dogs in the same*'). Here again is a striking dramatic contrast. Having affirmed the validity of the idea of deliverance with the grand Ex. 12, Brian now drives home the barbarity of glorying in vengeance, which – as the Psalmist suggests in this short but bloodthirsty verse – is its complement. Brian's setting of the verse falls into 3 sections, none of them comfortable listening, which together go to make up a single macabre *Allegro.* The first section begins with an ostinato in the strings, sly fragments of tune, and a kind of ghastly jollity in the vocal parts, which at first are entrusted to female voices alone. It gathers momentum with a glinting 3-note ostinato accompaniment on harps, celesta, flutes and muted trumpets. A new trumpet figure leads off the second section, which begins in F minor and is decorated with wry descending scales from the xylophone. The third section begins with a writhing 2-part ostinato pattern on violas and cellos:

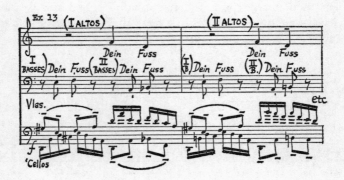

And proceeds to a climax of cruel merriment via a striking fanfare-like canon for voices and brass:

The climax is hardly past before the next episode bursts upon our ears in a blaze of brass and percussion.

'*Man seiht Gott . . .*' ('*They have seen thy goings, O God; even the goings of my God, my King, in the sanctuary. The singers went before, the players on instruments followed after; among them were the girls playing timbrels*'). The tempo is *Moderato ma pesante* and the victory-parade flavour is even more pronounced. A first stark march-like outburst in D minor is followed by a peremptory trumpet fanfare over side-drums and organ pedals, and leads to a sweeping passage for choirs and orchestra over a timpani ostinato. The militaristic overtones increase with a harsh brass tune, and the sweeping march that accompanies the entry of '*Die Sänger*'. Jubilation and naked force seem inextricably bound together now. Eventually, brass alone hammer home a massive cadence from A major into C, for the next episode.

'*Lobet Gott den Herrn . . .*' ('*Bless ye God in the congregations, even the Lord, from the fountain of Israel. There is little Benjamin with their ruler, the princes of Judah and their council, the princes of Zebulun and of Naphtali. Thy God hath commanded thy strength: strengthen, O God, that which thou hast wrought for us. Because of thy temple at Jerusalem shall Kings bring presents unto thee. Rebuke the company of the spearmen, the multitude of the mighty, till everyone submit himself with pieces of silver: scatter thou the people that delight in war*'). This long section of the Psalm is set rapidly, around the key of C minor. The mood of a barbaric procession has been unshakeably established, and the music knits itself tightly around a terse yet grandiose figure:

which is first cousin to Ex. 3*a* from the first movement. There is also a new rejoicing theme introduced by flutes, oboes, and oboi d'amore and this too relates to Ex. 3.

Ex 16

The choral writing, as if in response to Ex. 16, becomes full of semiquaver passage-work. The section breaks off with forceful repetitions of Ex. 15.

   '*Die Fürsten aus Agypten werden kommen . . .*' ('*Princes shall come out of Egypt; Ethiopia shall soon stretch out her hands unto God*'). The signature changes to 6/4, the mood to *Solenne*. Three quiet E major bars for organ, harps, glockenspiel and strings lead into C major and a paragraph of real majesty, scored for full chorus, the aforementioned instruments, and brass. The music has a familiar ring that may not at first be recognisable. The complex choral texture, the counter-melodies, and the fact that C major is soon abandoned for a move through distantly related keys, disguise the grand strong tune that is the backbone of the passage; but it is always found in at least 2 voice parts, reinforced by brass instruments. The tune itself goes through many transformations, though its first strain corresponds closely enough to its famous original:

Ex 17

Die   Für——sten   aus——   Ä-gypt-en   werd-en   kom—men

Here, in fact, is a chorale-variation on *Ein' Feste Burg* in multiple counterpoint of a complexity that Bach, Brahms, or even Reger hardly approached. Its use in this context is natural enough, but it also serves as another index of the work's specifically Germanic content. It culminates in a multi-voiced canon on the last phrase of the tune, and pauses on the dominant of A flat; it is typical of Brian that the next chord should come from the opposite end of the tonal spectrum – a new, victorious transformation of Ex. 1 breaks out in D major as a curtain-raiser to the next section.

'*Ihr Königreiche auf erden . . .*' ('*Sing unto God, ye kingdoms of the earth: O sing praises unto the Lord, to him that rideth upon the heavens, which were of old: lo, he doth send out his voice, and that a mighty voice*'). From now on the music rises from one triumphant, overbearing climax to another – climaxes magnificent in themselves, but cumulatively apalling in their fierceness. This section is an *Allegro Moderato* with full orchestra, based on Exx. 15 and 16 – the former soon becoming a driving ostinato in the bass. Before long the violins turn Ex. 16 into a rising sequence which ascends to –

'*Gebet Gott die Macht . . .*' ('*Ascribe ye strength unto God: his excellency is over Israel, and his strength is in the clouds. O God, thou art terrible out of thy holy places: the God of Israel is he that giveth strength and power unto his people*'). This is an *Andante Maestoso* in 12/8, and functions as a recapitulation of the 'military' music that followed Ex. 11. At least it returns to the general style of that section, and there is some literal recapitulation in the voice parts, using the new text. But a new figure

Ex 18

(plainly related to Ex. 15) becomes all-pervasive. The first statement of the verses gives way to a stormy orchestral episode based on it; and there follows a second statement which, beginning quietly on voices, harps, and strings, soon rises to a full-throated climax dominated by Ex. 18. Swinging repetitions of the words '*Macht und Kraft*' (good totalitarian values) lead to a *fff* brass outburst and an ascending chromatic scale for strings and woodwind. At its peak, the rhythm of the symphony's opening, Ex. 2, bursts in in E major. But it carries a tune no longer – its brazen harshness is laid bare. After 2 bars on brass and percussion it slips almost casually into C; and the work ends, to a thunderous '*Gelobt sei Gott!*', in a gigantic, deafening, bloated C major cadence for full choirs, organ and orchestra – victorious indeed, but also self-righteous, and pitiless.

That is Havergal Brian. Utterly. That is what he represents – music of heroic objectivity, with no illusions about man's inhumanity to man. The hollow splendour of human triumph has seldom, if ever, been more powerfully conveyed than in his

Fourth Symphony. Without the painful realism of this dark masterpiece, the dogged courage, tenderness, and stoic resignation of Brian's later music would hardly have been appropriate, nor possible.

7 'Wine of Summer': Symphony No. 5 (1937)

Das Siegeslied marks the end of a kind of 'Sturm und Drang' phase in Brian's music. More than 3 years elapsed before the composition of his next symphony, which stands very much alone in his output. Meanwhile, he was not idle. The first half of 1934 saw him occupied in writing a Violin Concerto. Alas, the score of this work was stolen in Victoria Station on June 8th, and has never been traced. The composer soon despaired of recovering it and, since no sketches remained, he set to work to produce a Second Violin Concerto, incorporating such themes as he could remember from the First, but in all essentials an entirely new composition. It was completed exactly a year after the loss of the First.

Only now does there seem to have been a gap in Brian's creativity. The Second Violin Concerto is a definite step towards simplification of form, material, harmony, and texture, and he may have felt the need of a pause to consider the direction his music was taking. Perhaps he simply desired a rest from strenuous creative work – after all, the large-scale works of the past 5 years represented a prodigious effort for a man in his late fifties. It was some time before he returned to composition: and the idea for his next symphony came to him indirectly, in connection with song-writing.

In early 1937, Havergal Brian was looking through the collected poems of Lord Alfred Douglas, with the specific purpose of finding something suitable for song-setting. He was a great admirer of Douglas's sonnets, but what most took his fancy on this occasion was a substantial poem entitled 'Wine of Summer', which seemed to invite large-scale treatment with orchestra. At first he thought of such a work as a Solo Cantata, and wrote to

Douglas requesting permission to use the poem. Oscar Wilde's 'evil genius' – poet, litigant, and memoirist – now in his sixties, seems to have been flattered by the proposal, and invited Brian to lunch to discuss it. Rather surprisingly, the two very different men established cordial relations, and Douglas gave Brian express permission to set as many of his poems as he liked.

Brian immediately began sketching his 'Solo Cantata'. It was roughed out in vocal score by April 8, 1937; and soon afterwards Brian visited Douglas in Brighton and played and sang the completed sketch through to him. Apparently the poet was enthusiastic and, fortified by his approval, Brian proceeded with the full score, completing it on June 18, 1937. The finished composition was no longer designated a Cantata but a 'Symphony for Solo Voice and Orchestra': a justified change of nomenclature in view of the work's unusually high degree of formal unity. It is fortunate that Douglas enjoyed Brian's impromptu rendering, for he was never to hear the symphony in any other form. *Wine of Summer* has yet to receive a professional performance; but the premiere took place with partly amateur forces at Kensington Town Hall on December 11th, 1969, with the baritone Brian Rayner Cook as a splendid soloist.

Although his disastrous association with Oscar Wilde will always keep the memory of Lord Alfred Douglas faintly green, his poetry – at one time widely admired – is now almost completely forgotten. 'Wine of Summer' was written in France, probably in 1897. If free from the worst excesses of 'decadent' Nineties verse, it is still very much of its period: a loose, rhapsodic effusion, its imagery distinguished by a fluent mixture of metaphors already half-dead. Its scheme – the recollection amid nature of a former delight in being alive, relapsing into present despair – had clear relevance for Douglas, who considered his life almost as blighted as Oscar Wilde's by the trials of 1895; but less clearly for Havergal Brian. Perhaps he saw a kind of parallel, in that he now pursued his vision surrounded by indifference, sustained by memories of his active involvement with music-making in the pre-War world, which was also Douglas's world.

At any rate, 'Wine of Summer' spurred Brian to compose some highly idiosyncratic music which responds neither to the diffuseness of Douglas's thought, nor his lack of verbal sobriety. It is in fact one of Brian's most austere works, at first sight almost perversely at variance with the poem's dreamy rhapsodizing. Its style is the reverse of 'Impressionistic'. Brian seems to eschew all merely pictorial relations between music and text, and all sensuous harmonic and colouristic effects. Instead the orchestral writing is barer than in any preceding work, the material plain to a degree, the thought sparely, almost severely contrapuntal, predominantly canonic in texture. The result strangely chastens Douglas's poem, countering its tired, careless imagery with a very precise train of pure, unclichéd musical thought that acts as both 'objective correlative' and emotional corrective – one even sometimes wonders if it does not function as a damning critique. The symphony is truly a meeting-ground of opposites. Brian does, at appropriate points, allow words and music to touch in onomato-poeic imagery: but he employs the standard evocative devices with an unromantic literalness, in a texture so starkly explicit that they cannot remain mere 'effects' – they must assume a structural, not a decorative function. Likewise the vocal writing retains little of the florid expressiveness of the solos in *The Gothic* and *Das Siegeslied*, but proceeds for the most part in a kind of heightened recitative. So if the symphony strikes a lyrical note, it is one of profoundly unsensuous lyricism.

In fact in its simplification *Wine of Summer* strongly anticipates the style of the later post-War symphonies. The orchestration, too, resembles their less extreme demands: triple woodwind (with a fourth flute); 4 horns, 3 trumpets, 3 trombones, tuba, strings, 2 harps, and (for Brian) a small percussion section of timpani, bass drum, side-drum, cymbals, glockenspiel and gong.

It is one of Brian's most closely-argued works. For the first performance, the 93-year-old composer contributed a short programme-note in which he clearly described the symphony as based on 'the theme announced by the soloist to the opening words of the poem'. This did not deter the critics from complain-ing that the work lacked any large-scale planning, even though the main theme (actually a double idea) is easy to distinguish, and with other organic connections, obviously determines the sym-phonic flow. *Wine of Summer* is in many ways a very plain-spoken work: its secrets have nothing to do with mere mystification.

The symphony opens with a slow orchestral introduction which sets the scene – the emotional scene, not the naturalistic one. There are no representations of the 'shimmering heat' in the poem: only an immense stillness and tension, the music seemingly poised immobile between opposite tonal poles. Reiterated violin figures and sparse harp notes are joined by a rising shape on bass clarinet and cellos.

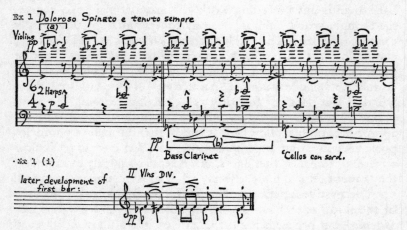

These first bars contain the seeds of the entire symphony. Their salient intervals – major and minor seconds, sevenths, and ninths, the minor third, the tritone, all expressive of harmonic tension – colour the whole work, both harmonically and melodically. The violins then begin a wandering motion, based on Ex. 1a, in parallel major and minor ninths; there is a solo horn-call, based on figure 1b; and then the voice enters.

> *The Sun holds all the Earth and all the Sky,*
> *From the gold throne of this mid-summer's day.*
> *In the soft air the shadow of a sigh*
> *Breathes on the leaves and scarcely makes them sway.*
> *The wood lies silent in the shimmering heat,*
> *Save where the insects make a lazy drone,*
> *And ever and anon from some tree near,*
> *   A dove's enamoured moan*
> *Or a distant rook's faint cawing harsh and sweet,*
> *Comes dimly floating to my listening ear.*

The theme mentioned by Brian has two halves, both capable of independent development. The soloist states the first in unison with cellos and basses, against an important quaver figure (*x*) which is itself developed extensively later in the work:

Figure *x* passes to full strings, pizzicato, while soloist, woodwind, and tuba state the second part of the theme.

At 'The wood lies silent . . .' the solo voice takes on a more recitative-like style, while fragments of Ex. 1 – particularly 1*a* – are heard in strings, woodwind, and horns. At 'harsh and sweet', figure *x* returns in the harps, and 1*b* in the cellos, and the conclusion of the verse leads to the first orchestral episode. This is a series of majestic, slow-moving canonic exchanges on rising figures for brass, low strings, and low woodwind, among which the shape of figure 2*a* comes and goes. Meanwhile the clucking figure *x* gradually spreads through the rest of the orchestra, until

a forceful canon on a descending-scale figure brings the music to
rest on a low pedal F. (While never attaining the status of a home
key, F is often used as a point of repose.) Over a drum-roll on
that note, the voice resumes.

> *Right in the wood's deep heart I lay me down,*
> *And look up at the sky between the leaves,*
> *Through delicate lace I see her deep blue gown.*
> *Across a fern a scarlet spider weaves*
> *From branch to branch a silver thread,*
> *And hangs there shining in white sunbeams,*
> *A ruby tremulous on a streak of light.*
> > *And high above my head*
> > *One spray of honeysuckle sways and dreams,*
> > *With one wild honey-bee for acolyte.*

The soloist is accompanied in turn by solo cor anglais, bassoon,
and horn, with a variation of Ex. 2 which is taken up by the voice.
The mention of the 'scarlet spider' starts violins weaving their
own thread of semiquaver figuration, leading to a brief climax at
'shining', where the music does, for a moment, seem to blaze
with light:

Ex 4

As the example shows, this provokes an agitated violin solo that might depict the scurrying spider but (like the prominent tritone in the voice) serves more to suggest an underlying tension which the poem itself has not so far made clear. The tonality shifts uneasily from bar to bar, and continues to do so for the rest of this section.

> *My nest is all untrod and virginal,*
> *And virginal the path that led me here,*
> *For all along the grass grew straight and tall,*
> *And live things rustled in the thicket near;*
> *And briar rose stretched out to sweet briar rose*
> *Wild slender arms, and barred the way to me*
> *With many a flowering arch, rose-pink or white,*
> *   As bending carefully,*
> *Leaving unbroken all their blossoming bows,*
> *I passed along, a reverent neophyte.*

The tempo, slow-paced so far, quickens perceptibly. The voice is first accompanied by multiple entries of 1*a*, passing from strings to horns and woodwind. At 'And briar rose . . .', intertwining staccato semiquaver scale passages weave through strings, woodwind, and harps; and at 'And barred the way . . .' the music gains power, with repetitions of 1*a* and 2*a* in diminution in the brass, reinforced by woodwind trills, harp glissandi, and the addition to the texture of timpani, cymbals, and glockenspiel. But at 'As bending carefully . . .' the tempo slows once more: most of the orchestra play a smooth 2-part canon on Ex. 3, adorned with cascading scales, similar to those in Ex. 4, on flutes, clarinets, violins, violas, and harps. The canon ends, at 'I passed along . . .', in a dragging ostinato on bassoons, cellos, basses and tuba, built out of repetitions of figure 3*a* with the addition of the little descending semiquaver figure 4*a* in flutes, harps, and violins. The music slows, and comes to an expectant halt on a sudden loud chord of F.

> *The air is full of soft imaginings,*
> *They float unseen beneath the hot sunbeams,*
> *Like tired moths on heavy velvet wings.*
> *They droop above my drowsy head like dreams.*
> *The hum of bees, the murmuring of doves,*

The soft faint whispering of unnumbered trees
Mingle with unreal things, and low and deep
From visionary groves,
Imagined lutes make voiceless harmonies,
And false flutes sigh before the gates of sleep.

Now begins one of the most sheerly beautiful sections of the
symphony, though with one exception Brian makes little attempt
at pictorial representation. He begins with a new figure

which clearly derives from Ex. 1*b*. Though its constituent
intervals are subject to innumerable variations, its shape and
rhythm remain distinctive. Ex. 5 gently rises and falls on muted
cellos and bass clarinet, moving through various keys while the
soloist sings the first lines of the stanza to some of the most
lyrical vocal phrases Brian has so far employed. Meanwhile flutes,
oboe, cor anglais, horns, harp and glockenspiel play Ex. 2*a* in
turn, with muted violins and violas winding between their various
entries. At 'The soft faint whispering . . .', Brian introduces his
sole onomatopoeic effect: a development – (i) in Ex. 2 – of figure
x. Flutes, bassoons, harp and violins take up this figure, while
violas and cellos superimpose various patterns of trills and grace-
notes: the passage is extraordinarily evocative of rustling leaves.
   However, at 'And low and deep . . .' the texture changes to a
cool rippling demisemiquaver movement in flutes, harp, and
violins, beneath which Brian conducts two canons on Ex. 2: the
first in woodwind and strings, the second (over a quiet pedal F in
timpani and basses) in the brass. The low pedal persists as the
rippling motion changes to a quiet swirling in the cellos, introducing the symphony's central section.

O rare sweet hour! O cup of golden wine!
The night of these my days is dull and dense,

And stars are few, be this the anodyne!
Of many woes the perfect recompense.
I thought that I had lost for evermore
The sense of this ethereal drunkenness,
This fierce desire to live, to breathe, to be;
*　　But even now, no less*
Than in the merry month that danced before
My tedious night, I taste its ecstasy.

Taste and remember all the summer days . . .

This is the heart of the poem, for better or worse, and Brian silences any doubts about the quality of the words by the splendid onward surge of his music. He begins by combining the voice with an emotional violin solo, which opens with a variant of Ex. 5 (its rising fourths and fifths altered to tritones) and proceeds to fervent octave double-stopping. Then, at 'I thought that I had lost . . .', he begins to build the work's central climax. For almost

the first time, the full power of the orchestra is brought into play. The soloist's phrases sweep higher, becoming more declamatory, while the orchestral fabric is built out of 1a and 2a in augmentation and diminution, with rising-scale passages in strings, bassoons, horns and tuba. The music grows wilder, until at last Brian gives it an emotional outlet. For once in this symphony whose thematic resources are normally so closely husbanded, he looses a sweeping, passionate outburst of melody (Ex. 6).

The tune is never to return. Here another practice of the later symphonies is foreshadowed: a sudden, brief melodic flowering, placed with uncanny skill to give the maximum emotional relief through respite from tight motivic work. Yet Ex. 6 also illustrates Brian's restraint and ability to keep power in reserve. For the dazzling modulation from F minor to E major at 'days' does not lead, as in some lesser composer it might, to an orgy of E major brightness. A single, gleaming chord suffices, and its lustre dies even as it sounds. There is a pause, and then bare woodwind and string sonorities tell of the illusory nature of Ex. 6's fulfilment.

> That lie, like gold reflections in the lake
> Of vanished years, unreal, but sweet always;
> Soft luminous shadows that I may not take
> Into my hands again, but still discern
> Drifting like gilded ghosts before my eyes
> Beneath the waters of forgotten things,
>   Sweet with faint memories,
> And mellow with old loves that used to burn
> Dead summer days ago, like fierce red kings.

At 'soft luminous shadows . . .' the voice returns to a recitative style over a throbbing rhythmic figure on muted second violins (a clear development of the opening bar of Ex. 1, and shown in that example), while solo woodwind sadly pass figure 2a between them. At 'faint memories', however, a sudden descending flute roulade brings a change of motion and atmosphere. There are brief, agitated violin and cello solos as the tempo fluctuates between *Lento* and *Allegro*; and then for the first time the music moves towards a real *Allegro* tempo with a marching rhythm on horns and harps, accompanied by a variant of Ex. 5 on solo flute echoed in inversion by solo double bass. The music quickly gathers force, and at 'fierce red kings' full brass, timpani, and unpitched percussion enter, culminating in a furious tattoo that introduces a violent orchestral episode.

The violence, however, is anything but undisciplined. Amid a timpani ostinato and trumpet-calls, the violins keep up a syncopated rhythm in major seconds, while cellos and basses nag away at alternating thirds, fifths, and tritones. Then trombones, tuba and horns give tongue with a fanfare (actually developed from figure *x* – see (ii) in Ex. 2), heralding the approach of – what cataclysm? No explosion, in fact, but a grim passage of constructive power whose ferocity lies in its uncompromising nature. Brian simply begins yet another canon on the Ex. 2 melody in woodwind and brass, with entries at 6 different degrees of the scale. Its starkness is accentuated by the harsh counterpoint, the passing discords softened by no chromatic alteration of the theme. But this canon leads to another, yet more complex: a steely web of dissonance spun out of the theme in combination with its retrograde form – a multiple crab-canon which is the logical extreme of the symphony's lean contrapuntal flow.

The great mass of skeletal polyphony slows and quietens over another F pedal in the timpani; until that changes to F-sharp, in which key the episode fades out with a softly pulsing rhythm in the trombones, against a quiet, wide-spaced chord in strings, flutes, horns and trumpets.

> *And this hour too must die, even now the sun*
> *Droops to the sea, and with untroubled feet*
> *The quiet evening comes: the day is done.*

The air that throbbed beneath the passionate heat
Grows calm and cool and virginal again.
The colour fades and sinks to sombre tones,
As when in youthful cheeks a blush grows dim.
Hushed are the monotones
Of doves and bees, and the long flowery lane
Rustles beneath the wind in playful whim.

One bar's transition on cellos and basses leads from F sharp to
E flat minor. The music begins to assume the character of a
recapitulation. The throbbing major seconds sound alternately in
horns and violas; the harps have form (iii) of figure x; flute and
oboe calmly play Ex. 3, while the soloist maintains the recitative-
like vocal line and a quietly-recurring gong-stroke hints presumably at the coming of night and the nearness of the sea. At 'The
air that throbbed . . .' there is a nice piece of musical imagery: the
music, still carried by the 'throbbing' seconds, grows momentarily
tense and chromatic, only to emerge into innocent diatonicism at
'virginal again', with a tranquil dialogue between solo flute and
horns. At 'The colour fades' the soloist is accompanied by muted
strings, with a canonic development of 1a. Then a pause, before
7 woodwind instruments – 4 flutes, 2 oboes and cor anglais –
softly spell out a descending whole-tone scale, each holding one
tone to create a glowing note-cluster. Here is the music's extreme
point of involvement with major seconds, and its extreme point
of stillness. Four times this simple, beautiful effect is repeated,
each quieter than the last, so that the final entries are actually
marked *ppppp*. They do not sound a fifth time: instead the soloist,
unaccompanied, sings 'Hushed are the monotones' to a descending-scale phrase, which avoids overstatement of the obvious by
not being a whole-tone one. Muted strings re-enter, and for 'the
long flowery lane' there is a brief return of rustling sonorities,
though without literal repetition of the earlier passage.

Gone are the passion and the pulse that beat
With feverish strokes, and gone the unseen things
That clothed the hour with shining raiment meet
To deck enchantments and imaginings.
No joy is here but only neutral peace
And loveless languor and indifference,
And faint remembrance of lost ecstasy.

> *The darkening shades increase,*
> *My dreams go out like tapers – I must hence.*
> *Far off I hear night calling to the sea.*

The music now moves towards its final climax, and again, as at the work's centre, there is a tendency to impassioned lyrical flowering, though with no recall of Ex. 6. The soloist declaims the first line *con passione* against ejaculatory brass outbursts, and the second to a rising phrase accompanied by another variant of *x* in the violins. Two fortissimo bars for full orchestra lead to a momentary calming, with horns quietly echoing against *2a* in cellos, harps and woodwind, before a last outpouring of expansive melody for the voice to the words 'No joy is here', accompanied by a final variant (iv) of *x*. Marching crotchets on bassoons, cellos, basses, trombones, and tuba come to rest on a pedal C-sharp, and the throbbing major seconds briefly reappear on two clarinets while solo woodwind sing *2a* for the last time, echoing the 'faint remembrance of lost ecstasy'.

There is a silence, and then the 2 harps enter with *x* in its most primitive form – a single oscillating octave A. Against this inner pedal, full strings, low woodwind and tuba play a quiet, darkly sonorous version of Ex. 3 while the soloist intones the closing lines of the poem. After 'my dreams go out ...', a swelling octave D on the horns introduces the final climax. Against thunderous rolls and crashes from drums and gong, the rest of the orchestra plays distorted fragments of Ex. *2a*, and the soloist must ride the tumult with as much power as he can command. It is a difficult task, but not impossible. These last few bars should conjure up a vision of great roaring breakers, almost – but not quite – overwhelming the singer's voice. If such a scheme has little connection with Douglas's lines, perhaps that is all to the good. The effect makes the end of *Wine of Summer* grimly, even histrionically dramatic, testifying to a depth of feeling hardly plumbed by the poem itself.

8 'Sinfonia Tragica': Symphony No. 6 (1948)

The 11 years that elapsed between *Wine of Summer* and Brian's next symphony are 'underground' years in his development. He was not idle – he was engaged in his largest work of all. But we are unable fully to judge that work, especially in relation to the music which came after it. This is *Prometheus Unbound*, a 'Lyrical Drama' for concert performance – a complete setting of Books I and II of Shelley's poem for many soloists, large choral forces, and huge orchestra, which would play for over four hours. Brian wrote it between 1937 and 1944.

Prometheus was clearly a crucial, and perhaps in intention a crowning work, taking up the challenge of a text that Brian particularly admired. That it was a very personal undertaking is clear from the manuscript vocal score, which became a kind of diary in which he entered such things as details of the weather and deaths in the family, along with the day's quota of music. Some commentators have opined that the result may be an impossible inflation of all the most grandiose elements of *The Gothic* and *Das Siegeslied* – a dead-end piece of musical extravagance created when he was 'musically at his lowest ebb'. But this is impossible to tell, for the full score is another missing Brian manuscript, and the vocal score gives little idea of the orchestral style of the finished work. In my opinion it seems much more likely that *Prometheus* further develops the spare, lean style of *Wine of Summer*. Certainly some of the thematic material has similar qualities, and such a development is a reasonable assumption, unless the works which followed constitute a complete artistic *volte-face*.

For three years after writing *Prometheus* Brian produced nothing new. He passed his 70th year and seems himself to have thought he would compose no more. But in 1948 his creative impulse burst forth again in a series of works which began the enormously rich harvest of the next 20 years. The first fruit of this 'late period' was the *Sinfonia Tragica*, completed on February 28, 1948, but probably begun during the preceding year.[1]

As explained earlier, the *Sinfonia Tragica* originally bore no number, and stood apart from the main symphonic canon until in 1967 it became Symphony No. 6. The reason for this anomaly has only recently become known. The work was always said to be 'inspired by J. M. Synge's tragedy *Dierdre of the Sorrows*'; but in a letter of 1970 the composer revealed that it was not planned as an independent work at all but as the *vorspiel* to an opera on that subject. It appears that he had been greatly impressed by a reading of Synge's works and especially the story of Dierdre – who, intended as the wife of the crafty king Conchubor, elopes with the young chieftain Naisi, and after Naisi is murdered under safe-conduct by Conchubor, commits suicide. Brian began work on a prelude at once and meanwhile applied for copyright permission to use Synge's text. It was refused – at the request of the Arts Council of Great Britain. The reason? They had already commissioned an opera on the subject from Karl Rankl, then Musical Director of Covent Garden, for the Festival of Britain.[2]

It was a bitter blow for Brian. Cutting his losses he finished the *Sinfonia* as a concert work. We do not know if he had written any of the opera proper, if any of it now survives, nor if the plan of the original Prelude was enlarged to include any of the opera's material. However, the *Sinfonia* is so complete in itself, seeming to encapsulate the essence of Synge's drama, that one wonders if a whole opera could have said more. The work is a true symphony, and a symphony of a new kind, marking a revolution of form and content only partially foreshadowed in Brian's earlier works. It is a masterpiece of expressive concision, attaining its powerful effect by bare suggestion, by a minimum of material and texture, in which every note has its place. The slim, 34-page score gives the impression in its 18 minutes of a work twice as large.

[1] The sketches of the *Tragica* are undated, but those of the next work, *The Tinker's Wedding* (completed March 6) are dated 27 January 1948. It seems Brian composed *both* works in sketch before beginning the *Tragica* full score.
[2] It is ironic that Rankl's opera, duly written and believed by some to be his finest work, has never been performed.

Another feature of this new departure is the orchestration, modest by comparison with all previous symphonies save *Wine of Summer* (triple woodwind, 4 horns, 3 trumpets, 3 trombones, tuba, harp and strings), apart from the percussion section. Here we find timpani, glockenspiel, xylophone, tambourine, cymbals, gong, castanets, bass drum – and also *three* side-drums, working in unison. From now on this 'trio' (a single drum cannot produce the same heavy yet penetrating sound) is an integral feature of Brian's orchestra.[1]

The form of the *Sinfonia Tragica* is a unique conception, an almost exact balance between a true one-movement symphony and a 3-movement form. There are three distinct sections: a substantial central slow movement framed by a brief introduction and a concentrated finale-plus-epilogue. Yet the music is continuous, thematic material is shared between sections and each passage grows logically from the previous one to produce a balanced, unified and wholly dramatic total form.

The tiny 'first movement' acts as an extraordinarily evocative prelude. It is the most economical music, sparing of matter and gesture, that Brian had yet written: everything is compressed and allusive, hinting at a mysterious world, awaiting great events. At the very opening it seems as if the music, already in motion long before, has only just come within earshot. For there is no preamble: the scurrying cello figures and high, cold woodwind cries admit us at once to a shadowy, haunted country of the mind.

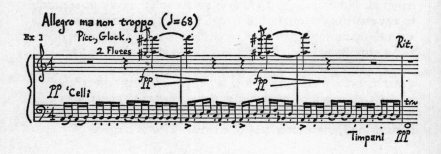

---

[1] The composer later suggested that the side-drum complement in most of his early works be raised to three also.

The tonality is ambiguous, though with a strong implication of
D minor which proves in time to be the work's main key. The
soft drum-roll at the end of Ex. 1 persists as the cellos resume the
nervous activity. Their opening figure contracts into an oscillating
semiquaver minor third, beneath which a solo tuba gives out a
sombre, faintly menacing theme that is one of the dominating
forces in the symphony:

Again the flow is interrupted: now by a still, long-held, tonally
equivocal chord for woodwind and divided basses and against
it there is a sudden splash of colour: a harp glissando, suggesting
E minor. A few quiet timpani-notes, like an echo of distant
thunder, settle on a drum-roll on B-flat. This is almost disembodied music, drawn with a few deft strokes and a minimum
of detail.

The cellos' restless motion resumes as in Ex. 1, shared between
all strings, and the woodwind cries return; but now a new element
is present, a far-off, fanfare-like trumpet call. It sounds twice in
the distance while the string phrases sway like reeds in the wind.
Who is this trumpeter, this note of humanity amid impersonal
nature? The music, of course, does not tell us. But a magical
sound-world has been conjured up: perhaps (for the trumpet-calls
are very similar) the very world that was glimpsed, briefly, in the
finale of Symphony No. 3.

Now bassoons, double bassoon, tuba and basses deliver the
solemn Ex. 2 against oscillating string minor thirds, exactly as
before (the static, unchanging nature of this and other principal
themes is a peculiar feature of the *Sinfonia*). Again the glowing,
equivocal chord interrupts, transposed a semitone lower, reinforced by brass and with the harp glissando suggesting F minor.
It dies away into the second half of the 'prelude', which begins
with a peaceful rocking semiquaver pattern on muted, divided
strings. Nothing ruffles the tranquillity save for a distant flurrying
trill on three muted trumpets, suddenly appearing as it were over

the horizon and vanishing again. After this, violins carry the rocking figure to the top of their register, against more distant thunder in bass drum and gong; and the symphony's first section closes on another bright, still woodwind chord and a slow harp arpeggio – the suggestion is now of D flat.

The slow central movement follows immediately; it begins with a new, sad theme on solo cor anglais:

It hardly seems an idea apt to symphonic development, yet Brian is able to use it often, with only slight modification, The oft-repeated initial note and the mournful 'tail' drooping across the vital interval of the minor third, have a greater power of suggestion than might be thought at first. In time they take on an air of primitive, indeed primeval, sorrow.

The cor anglais meditates on the shape of Ex. 3 in plangent unison with two low flutes – but almost at once the stillness is broken by a sudden accelerando and a thrusting bass figure stabs upward to a sharp climax. The upheaval lasts only a couple of bars, but it betrays the real passion beneath the music's surface. It dies out on a timpani-roll, with a solo horn-call sounding above the bass clarinet's resumption of Ex. 3. The orchestra takes up the theme and the pace increases to *Allegro Moderato*. Rising semi-quaver figures derived from Ex. 1 stream up through strings and clarinets while the flutes recall the earlier bird-like cries and muted trumpets add a shining halo of dissonance to the texture. The passage climaxes in a full orchestral outburst of canonic brass exchanges on the first bar of Ex. 2 and the upthrusting bass figure, with the martial heavy percussion noise of the 3 side-drums – their first entry.

The climax is cut short and the tonality, thus far unstable, now suggests E with a long-held, wide-spaced, bare-fifth chord on violins and basses. A wailing oboe phrase introduces another distant trumpet-call, with its touch of epic heroism and remote mystery. From the opposite direction comes an answer from a far-away horn, and then – in the intervening stretch of forest, so it seems – an innocent, bird-like call from a solo flute. This mingling of genuinely tragic feeling with a quality of fairy-tale magic is possibly unique to Brian – a distinctive element of his own personal sound-world.

After a pause, 3 flutes ('*unis.* but solo'), low in their register, sing out over a solemn, dragging crotchet rhythm in low pizzicato strings and harp, punctuated by the 3 side-drums. This leads, through clouded harmonies on bassoon, tuba, violas, cellos and basses, to the very heart of the symphony. Some have said that Brian is not, *per se*, a great melodist, and it is true that his symphonism is often at its most powerful and characteristic in the handling of brief figures which may be undistinguished in themselves. But the long theme that now unfolds on muted violins – infinitely sad, yet instinct with a nobility and tenderness of feeling that no words can convey – could only be the work of a melodist of the first rank and can surely stand comparison with the finest inspirations of Elgar or Vaughan Williams. I quote it almost entire, for its large scale and subtle asymmetry to be fully appreciated:

At first the melody is accompanied simply by the dragging harp-and-string crotchets of the preceding bars, and later more warmly and smoothly by trombones, tuba and low woodwind. Its peaceful last phrase (unquoted) is given to a solo horn. But almost at once the sorrowing Ex. 3 returns on solo woodwind, its entries marked *mistico*, and passes to a sighing music for muted, divided strings whose tense, wholly individual harmonies disguise a 5-part canon on a variant of the same theme. Ex. 5 shows the conclusion of the canon; and note how, by simply shifting the harmony up a semi-tone, Brian releases the tension and lightens the mood to one of gentle pathos, expressed by the flute's sad pastoral tune. The spirit is subtle yet the melody is very direct – and the scoring masterly in its economy:

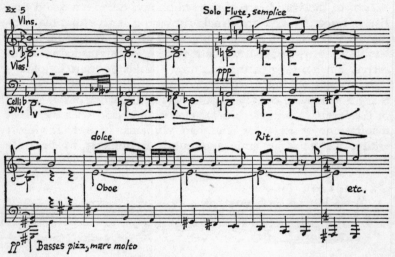

Now the great tune, Ex. 4, returns, more warmly and fully scored on woodwind, horns and strings, glorious and glowing in Brian's most affirmative key of E major and when it rises to a climax of calm ecstasy, it is hard not to think of Dierdre's 'seven years so sweet and shining, the gods would be hard set to give us seven days the like of them'. This is the expressive peak of the entire symphony. The climax comes with the appearance of figure 4*a*: here full brass, harp and glockenspiel enter and the phrase is repeated, lingeringly, as with wonderful sunset harmonies they dim the music's brightness from E major to C. Then, by another semitonal shift, the music is in C sharp, and Ex. 4 finally expires on a rising trumpet phrase, leaving 3 solo woodwind (piccolo, oboe and bassoon) to wander on together into the gathering shadows, their melancholy conversation gradually dissolving the salient characteristics of Ex. 3.

Muted strings re-enter and the pace increases. The woodwind cries of Ex. 1 return and against a rippling accompaniment from solo flute, harp and glockenspiel, the cellos sing out a wide-spanned, agitated melody:

Gradually it sinks to a low pedal D, and the key of D minor is confirmed by dark bassoon chords and a rising harp arpeggio. The violas, against trombone chords, passionately state Ex. 3, and the third part of the symphony begins abruptly with an angry brass and percussion fanfare, punctuated by a fortissimo 3-note timpani figure.

This 'finale' is scarcely longer than the prelude, yet so shattering is its release of energy that it feels like a really big *Allegro* movement. It makes subtle use of previous themes but drives to its violent climax with no hint of recapitulation. The structure is open-ended, swiftly and continuously developing, and if any one thing emphasizes structural unity it is the 3-note timpani figure: the idea of 3 notes constantly occurs, whether as a rhythmic ostinato or a punctuation-mark announcing a new section. But its form is always changing.

The preliminary fanfare gives way to a swelling tremolo crescendo on the strings, while the timpani go on the warpath with a whole battery of 3-note figures. This initiates a furious *Allegro* activity. Ex. 3 is the first theme to be recalled, its repeated notes now urgently syncopated in the strings, against *cuivré* horns and pounding timpani. Then the music plunges into a cacophonous tumult, with clattering percussion, pizzicato strings and trilling woodwind all in affray; and passes on to a strangely-scored dance-like section for high woodwind, muted trumpet and pizzicato strings accompanied by very light metallic percussion noises.

Trumpets and side-drums now set up a ferocious, dissonant, repeated-note ostinato in sextuplet rhythm, against which full strings, lower brass and woodwind grind out Ex. 2 in its most menacing colours. It culminates in a great cymbal-crash and a fury of grim elation as violins, harp and high woodwind whirl in a dizzy oscillation of minor thirds, and horns, cor anglais, violas and cellos passionately declaim a sonorous theme closely related to Ex. 2 and Ex. 6. This only brings further upheavals as the rest of the orchestra, with full percussion, batters against the melody in jerky, disruptive rhythms.

The pace quickens: horns and side-drums have a fresh 3-note pattern while strings, wodwind, glockenspiel, xylophone and harp swirl upwards in excited flurries of scales, tremolos and glissandi. A bassoon takes over the 3-note figure, rhythmically altered, and introduces a brief song for solo oboe against muted horns, reminding us of the prelude's bird-like cries. But almost at once this is brushed aside by a martial, fanfare-like rhythm in side-drums, oboes and clarinets. Against it, all bass instruments, horns and trumpets play a forceful, imperious, *deciso* canon on a descending-scale figure (derived by diminution from the opening phrase of Ex. 2). It spreads rapidly, angrily, through the orchestra; the various instruments scatter, as if trying to avoid disaster, in a cloud of semiquaver scales; and with brutal directness the catastrophe is upon us:

What is so uncanny is the way Brian makes the climactic C-major triad sound like a most devilish dissonance – never has that key been made more hostile! The energy of the movement now seems spent: the music slips wearily from C into D for a kind of exhausted epilogue in which a mournful cor anglais dwells on falling thirds over funereal trombone chords and then faintly recalls the beautiful Ex. 4.

Note how even here, in relative quietness, the percussion are an essential part of the texture – here, for the first time, they are beginning to play an almost continuo-like role in Brian's music.

After the last sombre brass chord has died away, timpani, bass drum and side drums continue for a little on their own, in soft pulsation.

The orchestra suddenly rouses itself with an upward-sweeping arpeggio and launches into a last glorious melodic flowering – *Lento e Solenne, molto sostenuto ed espressivo*. It is a rising tide of quiet melody in D minor, nobly tragic in mood and yet with a profoundly affecting sense of triumph. Only the words of poetry, not of description, can match its effect – most fittingly, perhaps, those of Synge's heroine at the point of death: 'I have put away sorrow like a shoe that is worn out and muddy, for it is I have had a life that will be envied by great companies .... It's a pitiful thing, Conchubor, you have done this night in Emain; yet a thing will be a joy and triumph to the ends of life and time.'

In that same spirit of solemn exaltation the music ascends to a rich cadential chord of D major, in which we hear a soft march-rhythm in trumpets and timpani and a ticking ostinato, like the beat of time itself, from harp, glockenspiel, xylophone, bass drum, side-drums and cymbals. From that background, on the violas, Ex. 3 arises for the last time, like an incantation – unchanged, in D minor, with its note of ancient sorrow. Then only the percussion ostinato remains, until a single mysterious gong-stroke extinguishes all other sounds and the echoes die into silence, and a kind of peace.

9 Symphony No. 7 in C major (1948)

1. *Allegro Moderato*   2. *Allegro Moderato ma Maestoso*
3. *Adagio – Allegro Moderato – Adagio*   4. *Moderato*

The *Sinfonia Tragica* was just the beginning of an immense renewal of creative activity. Within a fortnight of its completion Brian had finished a comedy overture inspired by another Synge play, *The Tinker's Wedding*, and a few days later he began a new symphony, his Seventh. It occupied him from March to September 14, 1948. Once complete, the work had 20 years to wait for its first performance.

This, Brian's last really large-scale symphony, with a playing-time of over 40 minutes, is scored for a slightly larger orchestra than the *Tragica*. The brass section includes a fourth trumpet and the percussion comprises glockenspiel, xylophone, celesta, cymbals, triangle, tambourine, bass drum, 3 side drums, gong and two deep-tuned bells (in C and E). The work is ostensibly in four movements. The second is a kind of moderately-paced scherzo; the third, which the composer himself considered as two movements 'involved with each other', consists of a second scherzo and a slow movement forming a single organic structure. The finale carries the title 'Epilogue – Once upon a time', which betrays an extra-musical impulse in a symphony that is otherwise wholly satisfying as 'pure' music. In a letter to the present writer, Brian identified this impulse as follows:

[No. 7] is an English Symphony on a German Subject much as *Hamlet* is an English play on a Danish subject . . . (it) came into existence after my reading Goethe's Autobiography . . . and that part which dealt with his life in Strassburg as a law student – his love for the Cathedral and other loves. Life was full and exciting for him.

All the more strange when once he left Strassburg for Weimar where he lived all his life, he never returned to Strassburg – hence 'Once upon a time'. . . .

The last note in the Symphony, E, is the actual sound of the great bell of Strassburg Cathedral.

As with Brian's other literary 'catalysts', it is pointless to use this one to trace detailed programmes in the music. This 'Symphony on a German Subject' is in fact in melodic accent one of the most 'English' of all his works. 'Life was full and exciting' might well stand as motto for the buoyant vitality of the first two movements. But after that the uncomplicated mood gives way to something deeper and stormier, expressed in sometimes tragic accents: the music moves on into a wider range of experience and in the end attains only a precarious calm. We might, in the most general terms, describe it as music which passes from Youth into Age: but its variety and complexity forbid us to go further.

Much of the work's tonal argument is concerned with the co-existence, or opposition, of C major and A minor. Conflicts between and ambiguities about relative major and minor are a highly characteristic feature of Brian's tonal language. (The reader will recall, for instance, the E flat minor/G flat major climax of *The Gothic*'s slow movement, the E major/C sharp minor tendencies in the *Te Deum* and the B flat minor/D flat major culmination of the scherzo of No. 2). In the first two movements of No. 7, A minor seems to function as an 'alternative' home key without tension; but later stages of the work bring a less easy relationship and the conclusion is not in C at all, but in A major.

The symphony begins with a striking call to attention. Two bars of rhythmic preparation in cymbals, bass drum and side drums provoke the first trumpet into virtuosic action and it is soon joined by the other 3 trumpets in a brilliant and ebullient

fanfare, affirming C major with absolute certainty. At the height
of their jubilation the trumpets stabilise on an expectant dominant
chord; the strings of the orchestra rouse themselves to life and
the main body of the movement opens with a massively confident
statement (Ex. 1).

Brian's symphonism is gaining succinctness all the time: these
six bars constitute almost the whole thematic material of the
movement. They contain three distinct ideas (*i*, *ii* and *iii* in
example), all making use of the rhythm *x*; and from these quite
simple materials Brian proceeds to build a complex and original
structure. Basically it is a kind of mosaic, whose individual fragments derive from the opening scale (sometimes an arpeggio) of
Ex. 1*i* and the strongly rhythmic Ex. 1*ii*, while Ex. 1*iii* provides
more decorative patterns. These fragments are woven together,
combined, juxtaposed and impregnated with each other's characteristics and thus are built into larger periods which go to make
up the outer sections of a concise yet weighty ternary form. It is
a process of variation which gives plenty of opportunity for
the use of root-and-branch metaphors, yet is flexible enough to
accommodate at least an echo of sonata form. Brian is able to
provide the spirit of exposition, second subject and recapitulation,
while disregarding their letter entirely. And then to confound all
labels, at the centre of the movement is a quiet episode, thematically unrelated to anything else, which is yet an essential part of the
scheme, for it throws the busy outer sections into relief.

This kind of literally bar-to-bar development is better heard in
all its vigour and excitement than wordily described and I shall
merely pick out the movement's most salient events. Ex. 1
initiates the stream of development and the music soon passes
into the 'alternative' key of A minor until, in the manner of
things, we begin to feel the time ripe for a 'second subject'. Brian
obliges our expectations, but very much in his own terms. A
minor becomes the dominant of D, and in D minor cellos, basses
and low woodwind state a quietly confident march-tune. It is the
first melody of any length that we have met, but its intimate
connection with Ex. 1 is obvious:

Ex.2 Cellos, Basses, Bassoons

pp suave and gentle

Pussyfooting along – for this music can take its time when it wants, for all its concentration – the tune collects woodwind counterpoints and drives towards a brief climax on C sharp, signalled by the irruption of a more sternly percussive, but still affirmative march-music. That dies down, but the music retains its liveliness and passes into a close-knit development of familiar elements:

Here we see the fragments of the 'mosaic': 1- or 2-bar periods which nonetheless cohere to give a convincing sense of onward flow. Elements of all three components of Ex. 1 can be seen, as well as rhythm *x*. The contrapuntal combination of motives, the discreet canonic imitations, the sudden flowering of melody, are all characteristic of Brian's mature style at its most supple.

The music now moves with increasing grandeur through E major and A major until it returns to C, grandly rounding off the first span of the movement in the tonic with developments of Ex. 1*i*. But there is no sense of a formal close: the effect is more one of sleight of hand, for abruptly and unexpectedly we find ourselves in the movement's central episode.

This central section is quite unlike the music which frames it. It is quiet, withdrawn, through-composed and slow-moving – providing a relief and a strong contrast to the rest of the movement. On another level, it illustrates a typical duality in Brian's sound-worlds – one which has been foreshadowed in earlier symphonies, but which only now achieves full expression. It might be described as the relationship and implied conflict between a 'foreground' and 'background' – the former in this case being the energetic, martial, confident music, suggestive of busy human activity; and the other the meditative, self-communing, slightly lonely music which seems to qualify and define the limits of that less reflective humanity. Essentially they are functions of entirely different kinds of symphonic *momentum*. Brian's ability to combine the two – to accommodate music of an almost Brucknerian breadth within concentrated, restless, even epigrammatic movements, is one of his most astonishing – and disconcerting – achievements.

The central span begins with an air of having been surprised in mid-modulation, and steers on strings alone towards D flat, where a new melody is heard on muted horns, accompanied by bassoon.

Soon Ex. 4 is repeated, in D, on cor anglais, clarinets and bass clarinet. Now ensues an absolutely static passage: long-held notes in violins and woodwind, beneath which the bass moves in even crotchets, forming one-bar patterns whose outlines change subtly all the time. Nothing seems to be happening – yet the basses' casual touching on a multitude of harmonic possibilities creates a sense of scale, and expectancy. Gradually, led by the oboe, solo woodwind and strings mount by slow ascending figures to a brief outcry, lyrical and yet full of tension. There is a pause, and then another region of stasis opens before us. Violins, flute, oboe and cor anglais hold high pedals suggesting the dominant of C major. In the depths, the cellos meditate on another even-crotchet pattern, which descends sequentially and is taken over by the basses. A soft chord of A flat on trombones and tuba ruffles the calm, and a semiquaver roulade in the flute suggests C minor.

Suddenly, *Animato*, the final span of the movement begins, launched by heroic trumpets and horns, not in C but in A minor.

Again we have concentrated development of the Ex. 1 material, with plenty of blaring brass and martial percussion. There is no recapitulation of first-span events, nor any melody corresponding to Ex. 2: development continues where it left off. The tempo broadens somewhat for a series of antiphonal exchanges, between brass, woodwind, and strings, of derivatives of Ex. 1*i*. The percussion take an increasingly important role, culminating in a brief but fierce xylophone cadenza (doubled by the trumpets – this feature of scoring is becoming characteristic). The music appears to be sweeping into a fast climax, when its momentum is suddenly stilled by three grinding chords on trumpets and trombones which introduce the slow, massive coda. Though lasting a mere five bars, this conclusion manages to suggest great size, as if all the energy of the movement has suddenly congealed into a single massive statement: essentially it is an apotheosis of Ex. 1*i*, grandly and firmly in C major, with a plain and simple cadence to finish.

The second movement, which confirms the optimism of the first and carries it to new heights, is another ternary-form design with more orthodox elements of recapitulation. But it too features much continuous variation: this time on two contrasting motives, announced in the opening bars.

The tramping bass line *a* and the excited repeated-note figure *b* form, in fact, the basis of the whole movement, and they father numerous progeny. Both have a latent energy which informs all of what is, despite its '*moderato ma maestoso*', a genuinely high-spirited scherzo.

The two elements are swept up immediately to a full orchestral outburst, suddenly cut short. A soft drum-roll intervenes, and then, seemingly far away, we hear a gay elfin music on oboe and muted horns – a folk-like tune obviously related to Ex. 5*b*.

The tune is rounded off by the pastoral warblings of a solo flute; restated a fourth higher, it is followed by a chuntering solo bassoon. The magical little episode concludes with singing high B-flats on oboe, flute and piccolo soli.

The original tempo and the tramping 5a return. Now, however, there is a horn tune above it – obviously a close relation.

Almost at once violins take up figure 7a in slightly altered form and, to the accompaniment of clashes on the C bell, the music launches into high-spirited activity for full orchestra, introducing new derivatives of 5a which are good-humouredly bandied about, most prominently in exchanges between trumpets and xylophone and glockenspiel. The passage culminates in a fortissimo statement of 5a on full brass and strings, plus crashes on cymbals and the E bell.

The next section, in quicker tempo, is a strenuous development of motives related to 5a, passing quickly through a wide variety of moods and instrumental colourings. Eventually it arrives at a fanfare-like canon between horns and trumpets, which grows and grows until the full brass dominate the music in a great repeated-note crescendo that at last heaves itself into a massive statement of 5a on full brass, strings and percussion. Without warning, that dissolves into a new, nonchalant tune on solo oboe:

This is a derivative of Ex. 5*b*, and introduces the central section of the movement, which concerns itself with such derivatives to the exclusion of 5*a*'s family. Ex. 8 is taken up by the flutes and provokes a good deal of merry activity in strings and woodwind, not the least important feature being the emergence of a march-like dotted rhythm in the strings. Suddenly solo piccolo, accompanied by muted horns, gives out another relation of 5*b* which recalls Ex. 6 in colour and character. It merges into quiet, mysterious activity in the violins, which take up the dotted rhythm high in their register while the cellos attempt a march-like theme:

There are a few more bars of hushed, expectant preparation and modulation, and then the movement's jollity erupts in a loud and vigorous C major march – graphically evoking a brass band striding along with a great deal of good-natured clash and clatter. The subject-matter here is Ex. 8 (which makes a highly virtuosic trumpet tune) and Ex. 9. Yet soon there is another 'dissolve' (Brian is by now the complete master of these instant transitions) and the march abruptly fades into the distance in a new *misterioso* tune that is the final transformation of Ex. 5*b*.

A variant of 5*a*, faintly sinister on pizzicato strings, C bell and cymbal, breaks in to introduce the movement's last span, which is basically a much-varied restatement of the music that began with Ex. 7. Trumpets and trombones boldly take up what was the horn theme and initiate another optimistic sweep of development. As before, the culmination is a broad statement of Ex. 5*a*: the final one, in full brass, against joyful counterpoints deriving from 7*a*. The movement, and indeed the symphony, has attained its peak of affirmation: and the coda continues this mood, lifting the music effortlessly up to a resounding bare-fifth chord of C. Sustained, it grows gradually fainter, while the E bell confirms C major by sounding the third of the triad – five times, with pizzicato strings, each stroke fainter than the last, so that the effect is of the music receding into the distance.

So far the symphony has been a confident, even extrovert work: there has been no real conflict, no challenge to C major's supremacy, though there have been occasional glimpses of tension beneath the surface. But from now on a shadow falls across the music, a shadow which deepens throughout the last two movements. The first note of the third movement tells us that we have moved far from home: it is G-flat, and in the key of G flat minor, so far from the clear C major we have just experienced, a beautiful, mysterious horn solo sounds out over chill tremolandi in the strings. The theme is never to return: it acts as a slow introduction to the main movement, conjuring up a lonely new region of the imagination with its bleak echo-effect. The pianissimo rustlings of the string accompaniment are like a breeze stirring the heather on a bare hillside.

The movement is the longest in the symphony in size and duration (it lasts over 15 minutes); and structurally it is the most individual. Broadly it comprises two well-defined sections. The first is another scherzo – yet 'scherzo' implies movement, and although this piece has *activity* in plenty, momentum and direction are almost non-existent. That is its function: it is a scherzo which gets nowhere – a scherzo that runs on the spot. The second part is a serious and beautiful slow movement which, though racked by storm, probes and searches for a peace that is gained at least temporarily. They are not independent: the *Adagio* grows out of the conflicts and anxieties of the scherzo-section, and together they make up a single inevitable structure.

After the preludial horn-theme, the scherzo-section begins *Allegro Moderato* with a change of time-signature to 6/8 and more rustling figuration in the strings. Then over a nagging quaver rhythm on an E-flat pedal in the timpani, solo flute and oboe share a melancholy scrap of tune – which like the horn theme does not return. Instead mysterious trills and scales are heard in upper strings, over meandering pizzicato quavers in the cellos. The harmonic implications of these elements change gradually, but without any sense of direction. From such unpromising beginnings the music labours to bring forth something thematic.

The early stages of the process need not be followed in detail. The music moves in bursts and spasms, charging up and down scales over heaving basses, seizing on ostinati that refuse to lead anywhere, punctuated by percussion interjections, passing through a kaleidoscopic range of colour, becoming more and more agitated as its efforts seem frustrated at every turn. All that it manages to produce – as a focus of activity rather than a motive, far less a theme – is the idea of a descending second (y), a few of whose presentations are shown in Ex. 10.

This element first takes solid form when the hitherto restless music finds itself suddenly becalmed over a timpani pedal B, and the flute states Ex. 10*ii*, by an enharmonic change, in C flat – a real no-man's-land key. But then, in a 5-part texture of tremolo, *sul ponticello* violins, it attempts something more fruitful.

The figure z is the important element here: it is to prove as fertile a seed as y is barren. The contrast is of dramatic importance: nagging away at y leads only to frustration, whereas z proves the starting-point of a host of related ideas which can bring peace. But peace is not a reality yet. Almost at once the aimless scherzo-music is off again, busily achieving nothing. Perhaps it is searching

for a new key to cling to, and it does attain a kind of A minor – but
now this seems a much more severe region than in the first two
movements. The music rises to a short-lived climax, but is cut
short in full career, and gives way to a rather nervous attempt at
stability, led by the woodwind, who seem to have decided that E
major might be the key to aim at. Their effort is short-lived,
disturbed by fidgety pizzicato strings determined to renew the
hectic activity. And soon there is another bout of agitation, the
strings trying to make something of y in inversion, without
success. Again a climax is reached, and again it is cut off.

Now we hear the timpani beating quavers on E and B, which
are revealed as tonic and dominant when a new, more successful
'calming passage' burgeons on woodwind and horns. This is the
first point of repose – as distinct from stasis – that the movement
has attained, and it has two significant features: it begins with,
and develops from, z; and it is in E major. Thus z is revealed as
the chief agent of pacification, and E major as its proper field of
operation:

The sonority of clarinets, bassoons and bass clarinet low in their
registers, moving in close harmony, is a typical glory of Brian's
woodwind writing – these rich, brown, reedy sounds are an unmistakable trait. Ex. 12 grows and develops lyrically, as if to
suggest that the slow movement has arrived. It even pacifies y,
(as shown in Ex. 10*iii*), and it moves into a region of sheer

enjoyment of colour, with calm figuration on harp and glockenspiel. But the timpani have kept up their quiet, insistent quaver
beat – the scherzo rhythm is still there. And so once more the
agitation breaks out, into the most violent orchestral convulsion
yet. After the placid measures we have just heard, it has a night-
marish quality – this kind of music is obviously a dead end, but it
refuses to loosen its hold. Figure *y* is seized on, and the brass and
percussion inflate it into a vicious juggernaut (Ex. 10*iv*). The
music charges blindly onward in a series of ascending scales, as if
heading for some catastrophe. Suddenly it is cut off in mid-
stride. There is a single silent bar; then, with the serene power of
a benediction, the slow movement begins.

The transition is magnificently achieved. The scherzo's last
angry outburst is halted on the dominant of A flat; the silent bar
gives the listener space in which to develop expectations of that
key; and so the surprise, and the relief, is all the greater when
music shines forth from a different tonal direction – E major. For
in that radiant key the first 3 notes of *z* descend, as if from the
skies, on violins and oboe, over throbbing horn chords.

Almost at once the music turns to the minor, but the brief,
intense vision of E major assures us that we are clear of the
earthbound strife of the scherzo; we are, relatively, safe. Brian is
unusually specific about the character of these bars: in the score
he marks them 'Slow & sustained – powerful, eloquent, yet
tender'. The tenderness persists as first a double bass, then a cello
in canon with bass clarinet, lead into C minor. In that key begins
a beautiful, elegiac development. The texture is complex and
polyphonic, the main melody appearing in the violas, and extend-
ing in a long, fluid line derived from the premises of *z* and 12*a*:

Ex 13

This particular kind of long, rather florid, expressive line, associated as it is with a rich, meditative contrapuntal texture, seems strikingly prophetic of what we find in some of the slow movements of Tippett, both in technique and effect. Ex. 13 is presented at first in a 4-part texture; but as the melody rises and is taken up by the violins, the polyphony broadens out in richness and complexity to 10 parts, supported by the harp. In the midst of the ornamentation figure y creeps in, discreetly – now relegated to the much more suitable role of an accompanimental detail.

A figure of 3 descending notes, presented on horns and harp, next becomes the subject for discussion, and is taken up and elaborated in augmentation and diminution by solo harp, trombones, and a duo of solo violin and viola. All this has taken us very far from the E major of the movement's opening – so far, in fact, that the music is once more at the gates of A flat. The mood is still quiet and reflective, but it has grown darker, more shadowed. Two solitary, enigmatic blasts from muted horns come strangely to the ear. Discussion of the 3-note figure peters out. Both musically and atmospherically, everything has gone very quiet; the quiet before a storm. A solo horn gives out the opening phrase of Ex. 13 in D flat . . . .

And the storm breaks. The quiet is shattered by a terrific orchestral outburst, *vivo agitato* – the most violent convulsion in the whole work. Its fury and malice strongly recall the last stages of the scherzo-section: was this the cataclysm that the brief E major vision so narrowly averted? The full resources of the orchestra are employed, and the ferocity of the writing demands virtuoso execution. But in one important respect this passage differs from anything in the scherzo-section: it is strongly thematic. While side-drums, horns and trombones keep up a furious inner rattling, the music above and below this resolves into a gigantic canon, directly derived from z and closely related to Ex. 13. The main key is A minor, now very different from the casual 'alternative key' of the first two movements; and the culmination is a series of shattering, downward-jabbing, A minor scales – stark, austere and utterly comfortless.

The outburst peters out as quickly as it blew up, with disjointed references to y; and the calm of the slow movement somehow reasserts itself. The very violence of the cataclysm assures us that it cannot return; already the clouds are clearing. The tempo

becomes *Lento*; the violins give z a new downward-tending
shape; *y* is heard, tamed once more, as the strings steer through
some beautiful modulations towards – at last – E major. Woodwind and strings set up a peaceful, lapping rhythm as background
to a tranquil canon on the new shape of z, between cellos and
violins. The melodic line is similar in style to Ex. 13, though the
texture is less complex. A mood of deep peace is created, and at
the end of the canon, for a short time at least, tranquillity is
complete and the music sunlit again, stirred only by the lapping
rhythm. A solo violin now pours forth a long, quasi-improvisatory
stream of trills and demisemiquavers, decorating z and its
associated ideas in an ecstasy of cat-like contentment. It is a
wonderful moment – the emotional fulfilment of all that the long
movement has been searching for since the start. But it must pass.
The solo violin falls silent, and the mood darkens with the entry
of the trombones. The music attempts to regain its haven of
peace, with a new 'lapping' rhythm in the strings and figure z in
the woodwind. But the key is now G minor, no safe habitation.
The trombones take up the rhythm and colour it sombrely, and
the music ascends to a final, sustained bare-fifth chord of E flat,
against which the glockenspiel clashes in a soft ostinato, ending
on a D, against another bare-fifth, on C, from the harp – leaving
the tonal situation, in the end, thoroughly ambiguous.

In fact, the finale returns to the A-C relationship of the earlier
movements, but in a far more serious mood; it begins grimly in A
minor, with a march-rhythm on the horns that is the movement's
single most important element:

This 'Epilogue' is no mere rounding-off, but contains the
symphony's deepest music and its grimmest struggles. The
march-rhythm is never absent for long, and it conditions the
'journeying' character of the music as it incessantly probes and
explores.

The rhythm carries with it in Ex. 14 a melodic shape on the strings that is a hint rather than a theme in its own right. Further hints by woodwind and strings are soon confirmed by a warm, noble tune, arising from the richly sonorous combination of trombones, tuba and harp:

Only this once does Ex. 15 appear in its full form, but fragments and variants of it sound through much of the rest of the movement. Woodwind and strings meditate on it for a while, until there is a call to action – a fanfare-like motive from the whole woodwind body:

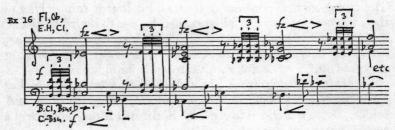

Abruptly the peace is shattered as a wild tutti breaks out, filled with battering percussion and disruptive cross-rhythms on the strings. With a rhetorical cadence-figure on the trombones, this warlike music crashes bodily into C – but C *minor*, the key of tragedy. As if to seal its doom, Brian goes to the trouble of marking a general C minor key-signature in the score – the only one in the symphony.

Now the struggle is on with a vengeance. Trumpets proclaim the march-rhythm on C, with trombones and side-drums; tragic variants of Ex. 15 are counterpointed against it on strings and woodwind, and above the tumult a new, grimly heroic horn theme is heard. The climax continues, spurred on by a new rhythmic figure in the strings, from which springs an impassioned, increasingly agitated violin line. Gradually the turmoil recedes, and calmer fragments of Ex. 15 appear in the strings. It is noteworthy that nearly all the material of this movement can be traced back to Exx. 14, 15 and 16 – but the thematic connections are much freer, more allusive, than would have been the case in earlier works. Only the march-rhythm is unchanging, forging relentlessly on.

Peace has not been restored: but a brief incursion of *pesante* march-music and trumpet flourishes is suddenly followed by a complete change of perspective – a trialogue of solo violin, viola and cello, on elements of Ex. 14, the viola taking the march-rhythm. Then all the violas, divided in 3, alternately arco and pizzicato, supported by the harp, quietly state the rhythm on its own. It passes to the timpani, while a melancholy new figure (significantly involving the interval of a falling second – remember figure *y*?) is heard on the woodwind.

Gradually the rhythm pervades everything as the music grows in weight and volume, and a new heroic version of the march bursts out on trumpets and strings. But the stormy climax thus provoked is short-lived, and gives way almost at once to a wailing passage on the strings in which we suddenly hear a ghost from the preceding movement – figure *y*:

Already presaged by the woodwind's falling-second idea, it strikes a note of weariness. March-music breaks in again, but it sounds merely harsh. Still, it passes: the harmony brightens, Brian cancels the general C minor key-signature, and a harp arpeggio seems to promise the arrival of C major.

A soft brass chord, however, turns the key to the 'alternative', A minor; and from this chord there springs a long violin solo, as at the high-point of the third movement. It is, perhaps, the most beautiful moment in the symphony: the solo writing is less florid

than before – simpler, more poignant, valedictory in mood, as if
the work is to be crowned by a serene farewell. But then the
violin, *con passione*, gives out *y*, and the rest of the violins take it
up in augmentation in a *molto sostenuto e cantabile* passage of
supplication.

Suddenly this is brutally cut off by a last furious outburst.
Shorter, less overpowering, but more vicious than the cataclysm
that rocked the third movement, it consists largely of angry
reiterations of *y*, spitting from woodwind and percussion, against
violent flutter-tonguing and trills in full brass. It blows itself out
almost as soon as it has appeared, but it seems to have banished
all hope of true peace. The brief coda follows, quietly: as at the
end of the *Tragica*, this is the quiet of exhaustion. All that the
outburst has left is a bare-fifth C-G on tremolo violins, ironically
suggesting C major at last with no sense of fulfilment. The march-
rhythm sounds again, bleak and remote, in horns and trumpets,
on A, implying A minor against the persistent C-G. A descending
sequence of falling seconds, stemming from *y* as it appeared in
Ex. 17, sounds sadly, low in the basses and high on solo oboe. It
ceases. The C-G ceases. Only a bare A remains. It seems the music
will slow down and end in comfortless A minor.

And then comes the last chord, scored for strings, trombones,
tuba and E bell: and it is a surprise – A major. We are still adjust-
ing to the surprise when, on a solemn gong-stroke, the music
melts at last into silence. This final unhoped-for A major might
be regarded as a kind of *tierce de Picardie*; but that is not its effect.
The chord stands as a thing in itself, not an inevitable conclusion
but a new entity. Worn out by struggles and with more than a
hint of disillusionment, the music is suddenly brought up short
by a phenomenon beyond its range of experience – this calm but
mysterious chord, with its strange bell. We do not need to know
it for the bell of Strassburg Cathedral; its point is that it opens up
new possibilities, when the whole import of the apparently inevitable A minor close was that no more existed. It suggests the
hope – not the certainty – of renewal. So Brian's Symphony No. 7
ends neither in despair or false optimism; but realistically, with
a new question awaiting answer.

Symphony No. 8 in B flat minor (1949)

Brian's one-movement Eighth Symphony followed soon after the Seventh. He began sketching it on January 25, 1949, and completed a pencil short score by March 27. A second, and final, short score in ink, incorporating several important alterations to the original design, followed by April 11, and Brian then set about constructing a full score, which was finished on May 17. Up to this time none of his symphonies had ever been performed, but with No. 8 his luck began to change. Only four years after its completion, the score came to the notice of a young producer of BBC orchestral concerts, on the lookout for unjustly neglected English works. His name was Robert Simpson; and he was so impressed and intrigued by this music – so different from anything he had encountered before – that he arranged for the symphony to be performed by the London Philharmonic Orchestra under Sir Adrian Boult. Brian, at the age of 78, had found his champion at last.

Simpson's interest was perhaps sparked so strongly because his first contact with Havergal Brian was through one of his toughest and most uncompromising works. The *Sinfonia Tragica* certainly signals a new departure in its economy and concentration of thought, but in other respects (the static nature of the themes, for instance) it is stylistically somewhat isolated. The Seventh maintains the compressed mode of thought but within an expansive framework that recalls the pre-war symphonies. The Eighth is a much bolder step forward and propounds problems wholly in fresh stylistic terms which required two further symphonies to work out all the implications. Symphonies 8, 9 and 10 have in fact been called a 'trilogy' ('brothers', was Brian's own term) and

Symphony No. 8: a page from the manuscript
(Passacaglia I)

as long as we recognize that each work has its own distinctive character, that there are no programmatic connexions between them and that they relate as much to the two intervening operas (*Turandot* and *The Cenci*) as to each other, it is not inappropriate to view them so. In general terms one might say that No. 8 poses the questions; No. 9 grapples with them and wins through to an optimistic conclusion; but No. 10 challenges that conclusion's finality, and propounds a very much wider view.

Symphony No. 8 is scored for triple woodwind, 4 horns, 3 trumpets, 3 trombones, euphonium, tuba, timpani, strings, harp, piano, glockenspiel, xylophone, bass drum, 3 side drums, triangle, tambourine, cymbals, castanets and gong (and in 1971 Brian added an *ad libitum* organ part at the final climax). This is the last symphony to employ a piano in the orchestra and its use is very different from that of the piano duos in the Second and Third Symphonies. It may not be so virtuosic or obtrusive, but it adds a distinctive quality to the overall sound, both as a percussive melodic reinforcement and as a plangent anti-harp.

The autograph title-page carries the superscription 'Inspiration – die ballade *Die Braut von Corinth*' (another Goethean subject!); but later the composer was careful to describe the ballad as giving only an 'initial stimulus'. Of all the literary 'catalysts' in Brian's symphonies this one needs the most cautious treatment. There is simply nothing in the music to suggest any programmatic correspondence with Goethe's celebrated (if macabre) tale of the Christianized vampire who, already dead herself, drains the blood of her intended bridegroom. Indeed, to discuss it in those terms could only be trivialization. Brian himself was quite clear on the point when he wrote:[1]

> It is not illustration: if it were it would be a symphonic poem. And although it is not even a first cousin of classical sonata form, I consider that in structure it is as firmly based as Bach's great Fugue in B flat minor in the '48', which may remotely have influenced my work – we don't know.

Indeed we don't – there is certainly no obvious resemblance between the two works. (Yet it is significant that Brian should mention Bach in this context. His general influence on Brian's musical thought was, I believe, immense, and has not so far been

[1] to Reginald Nettel; quoted by him in 'The Symphonies of Havergal Brian *The Listener*, 28 January 1954, p. 197).

widely recognized). But Brian is certainly justified in his estima-
tion of the firm basis of the structure – one of the most unique and
original he ever devised. Broadly speaking, the symphony deploys
static elements, continuous metamorphosis of germinal figures,
and the permutation of 'families' of related themes, in a profusion
that is at first bewildering but is in fact highly unified; and all the
diverse threads of the argument are drawn together in two extraordinary, independent, but closely related passacaglias.

The richly organic nature of these processes is disguised by the
fact that the atmosphere is one of perpetual conflict and in this
sense only might we draw a parallel with *Die Braut von Corinth*,
which essentially symbolizes the struggle between the forces of
life and death. No other Brian symphony is so powerfully and
consistently based on the opposition of highly-contrasting
elements. Tender lyricism and militaristic harshness; deep stillness
and headlong momentum; the darkest and lightest textures;
upward-yearning and downward-sinking melodic movement;
perpetual variation and that which refuses to be changed – in all
respects, Symphony No. 8 is a battlefield of extremes, with no
middle ground and no final resolution.

Not unnaturally the work arouses mixed feelings. On first
hearing listeners tend to prefer one set of opposites to the other:
they respond strongly to the work's great lyrical moments while
resenting the harsh march-rhythms which seem to contradict
them; or they feel in those march-rhythms something urgent,
realistic and contemporary, while they associate the lyricism with
a more 'conventional' style. Only later do we come to see that the
extremes, far from cancelling one another out, each give the other
a greater reality than it could possess on its own. The beauty is
real *because* it is under attack and is forced to heights of wild
lyricism rare in Brian's output. The violence is real *because* it is
measured against something positive, giving us a standard by
which to judge its true power. Torn by this perpetual antinomy,
supercharged with strong emotions, the music generates enormous tension. Behind the tension is an implicit tragedy – that of
the irreconcilable impulses in human life.

None of Brian's symphonies has a stranger opening. A convulsive, almost uncouth march-music (Ex. 1*a*), approaching the
main key obliquely from G flat, is juxtaposed against a still bare-
fifth chord on B flat, deep and quiet as night, and a melodic

development of the chord – a solemn horn-call (Ex. 1*b*), full of
ancient mystery:

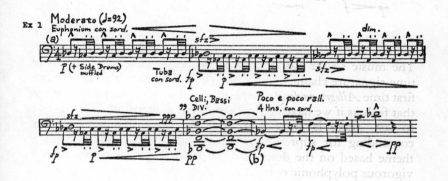

The rhythmic pattern of Ex. 1*a* is *the* archetypal 'Brian rhythm',
associated most strongly with the funeral marches that resound
throughout his music. In this work it grows in a number of ways
and is in fact one of the germinal themes of the entire design.
Ex. 1*b* is another seed, whose rising fifths, especially, are to be
widely exploited.

The grotesque euphonium-tuba-side drum march is resumed
and is again broken off. The B flat bare-fifth, now on low brass, is
heard anew; the horns restate Ex. 1*b*, and the piano quietly plays
a deliberate descending scale of B flat minor in even crotchets.
The scale is another vital element: the work's basic material may
be very simple, but it gives rise in time to processes of enormous
complexity. As the horns extend 1*b*, bass instruments state an
ostinato figure (Ex. 2*a* below) whose *falling* fifth links it with 1*b*.
Brian proceeds at once to develop this initial material – with
descending scales on tuba, harp and piano, 1*b* rising on euphonium and tuba, and variations of 2*a* in the strings; and then *rising*
scales in cellos and basses, an extended 1*b falling*, by inversion, in
the bass instruments, and 2*a* further developed in woodwind and
strings. Euphonium and tuba next introduce another short figure
(Ex. 2*b*) stemming from 1*a*, whose rhythm is hinted at by the
side-drums.

Ex 2

The music so far has had an introductory character. Now the time-signature changes to 9/4 and the full orchestra enters for the first time *Allegro moderato ma pesante e marcato*, in a majestic passage that feels as if we have arrived at a 'main movement'. But it is not to last – there is *no* main movement, only different elements contending for supremacy. The passage begins boldly with a theme based on the descending-scale idea and continues with a vigorous polyphonic complex in which the rhythm of Ex. 1*a*, the rising fifths of 1*b*, and figure 2*b* all play a prominent part. A climax, with rushing semiquaver figuration in B flat major, is cut off in mid-stride. Suddenly the music is back in B flat minor and the original tempo. Now Ex. 1*b* is varied in a long, slow, ascending line in the piano and deliberate falling scales sound low in pizzicato cellos and basses and high in harp and glockenspiel. Bass clarinet and bassoons vary 2*a* and a piccolo reinforces the piano's treatment of 1*b* in the highest register. The passage concludes in A minor with delicate, airy textures – oscillating octave E's (another important figure) in piccolo, piano and timpani; calm ascending and descending scales in bassoon, harp and pizzicato lower strings, reflective solos from cor anglais and horn and 2*a* lightly shared between flutes and violins.

Muted strings now have a tender episode to themselves. Against rising and falling scales in cellos and basses, the violins converse over a new figure that is closely derived from 1*a* through 2*b*:

Ex 3

But this calm is short-lived. After a brief clarinet solo the music erupts into action with an angry, martial episode built upon an obstinate bass figure like the sound of thudding hooves:

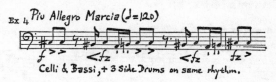

The contrast of character with Ex. 3 could scarcely be greater, yet Ex. 4's derivation is plainly similar – from 1a and 2b. Euphonium and tuba take up its galloping rhythms, but it peters out indecisively with developments from 2a in the woodwind, above a pedal E-flat in timpani.

Again comes a complete change of mood and texture. In D flat (B flat minor's relative major), violins and cellos give out a new, long-breathed, singing theme, which in contrast to the fairly simple material so far exposed partakes of some of the florid expressiveness we noted in the theme of the slow movement of Symphony No. 7. It is, if you like, a kind of 'second subject', but arrived at far later than would be the case in any sonata-scheme.

Its opening shape (x), the decorative swirl of notes which follows it and the prominent tritone in the third bar are all to be extensively developed later, as a strong contrast to Exx. 1 to 4. But even at this first appearance the theme is accompanied by the rising fifths of 1b, in the harp. And it lasts no longer than any previous episode. Instead, new material intervenes and for four bars a clanking march-music (*Accel. agitato subito* – a solo trumpet turns Ex. 4 into a minatory war-call above trudging chords in basses, piano and harp) alternates with a quiet string figure from which is soon to grow another theme. This gives way to a calm canonic dialogue in which 2 flutes, *teneramente*, converse in a variation of Ex. 3 over descending-scale figures in solo bassoon and harp.

The violas, supported by horns, follow with the new, gravely expressive theme foreshadowed by the string figure of a few bars earlier. New it is and yet it is also a distant, lyrical transformation of both elements of Ex. 1:

The theme is taken up more warmly by cellos and horns, but with murky harmonies low in basses, bassoons, euphonium and tuba. It flows at length into a series of tense, harmonically ambiguous wind chords, through which (as if through a mist) the first horn calls again and again with a falling octave G. The passage culminates in a sudden 7th-chord on B-flat, leaving the horn, alone, exposed on a high C.

We are near the mid-point of the symphony and it would not be inaccurate to regard all that has been heard so far as an immense 'exposition'. Though all the elements have been treated to or arrived at by, a certain amount of development, the *real* development – and the real conflict – lies ahead.

The solo horn now descends gradually from its high note in a line that develops the falling-octave figure. The euphonium joins it in quasi-canon, taking over the descending line and bringing it slowly down to a sustained low E. Beneath this the tuba puts down a B – recalling the bare-fifth of Ex. 1 but a semitone higher. Thus prompted, *1b* returns, in canon, on 3 bassoons, *molto sostenuto e mistico*. They extend and reflect upon it in reedy, nasal tones and conclude with another bare-fifth, on G.

Now the extremes are really brought to battle. The tempo becomes *Allegro moderato* and at first nothing can be heard but the distant hoofbeats of the Ex. 4 rhythm on muffled, softly-tapping side-drums. Then cellos and basses enter with Ex. 4 itself and the music suddenly launches into a furious, rushing *Allegro molto e agitato* in B flat minor. Trumpets take over Ex. 4, while the bass instruments charge on in semiquaver figurations derived from it; and the headlong drive climaxes in a wild, high, shrieking trumpet G against Ex. 4, pounding out heavily on side drums and horns.

There is a pause; a single poignant bar scored for harp, 2 muted horns, and a falling-fifth phrase on solo oboe; another pause. And then, *Adagio e molto espressivo*, comes the great central lyrical out-pouring of the symphony, bravely outfacing the implications of the harsh *Allegro* with full-hearted passion of an intensity rare even in Brian's music. It begins in E major – always, for him, the key of light and hope – as a canonic fantasia for full orchestra on a variant of Ex. 5. Ex. 7 shows the first few bars in somewhat simplified texture.

The falling fifth can be seen in the fourth bar and this (together with rising fifths) becomes an important element in the rest of the tremendous statement. But the main subject remains the derivative of Ex. 5, with its swirling demisemiquavers, and at length these bring the music to a tumultuous climax in E major that rises, with wrenching dissonance, onto the dazzling brightness of E *sharp*.[1]

---

[1] Brian notates it thus (i.e., not as F major) as if to suggest a kind of 'super-E'. This E major–E sharp progression is one he reserves for very rare climactic moments in his music (cf. Symphony No. 10, Ex. 6), and will be further discussed in a more general consideration of his harmonic procedures in Volume II. Its failure to win control here is, of course, a mark of the tragedy inherent in this symphony.

It is an overwhelming moment, but not even this can gain complete mastery. The climax is suddenly shut off and is replaced by a *lamentando* flute solo that sadly develops the falling-fifth figure as if to imply that such high endeavours are all hopeless in the end. The tension caused by the curt rejection of such powerfully affirmative music becomes almost unbearable: side-drums quietly beat out a new march-rhythm and violins and violas stab it out loudly, almost hysterically, *con fuoco e forza*. This outburst too collapses almost at once, but into assuagement: three bars of pacifying harmonies on harp and cellos in 5 parts lead into a wonderful episode. Against a fragile, delicate accompaniment of piano, harp and glockenspiel, plashing and rippling in chords, arpeggios and single notes, we hear a pale, lovely wraith of a tune on muted violins:

It is another variation of Ex. 5 (the opening, like that of Ex. 7, derives from *x*), but reduced now to absolute simplicity and tenderness. How different from the great slow melodies of the *Tragica* and Symphony No. 7 (Exx. 4 and 13 in the respective chapters) – and yet how plainly all three emanate from the same mind! Thus we see how a composer who may not be, '*per se*', a great melodist, can still be a great melodist, period.

Now comes a deeply moving 6/8 passage, based on a variant of Ex. 6. It begins hesitantly in tenebrous depths, on horn, bassoons,

double-bassoon and much-divided cellos and basses: but it grows
and grows, like a plant forcing its way through the soil, rising
through keys and timbres until it emerges into the light in airy,
floating semiquaver lines on flutes and violins. At this point a
strange, fanfare-like *gruppetto* of four notes is heard high on 3
muted trombones: a mysterious sound. What it forebodes is an
amazing Passacaglia – for the *gruppetto* rhythm is also that of the
extraordinary passacaglia bass theme, which follows at once on
cellos, bassoons and muffled side-drums.

The theme itself (Ex. 9*a*) has strong affinities with Exx. 1*a* and 4.
Above it Brian develops a web of flurrying hemidemisemiquavers
(which surely stem from Exx. 5 and 7) on muted violins. Ex. 9
shows merely the first bar of this process:

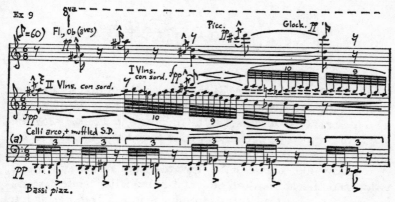

and it introduces one of the most intricate, original, and fantastic-
ally-imagined of all Brian's sound-worlds. Since the theme 9*a* is
itself only one bar long, every bar is strictly speaking an individual
variation; but Brian uses the separate bars only as the building-
blocks of larger structures and the Passacaglia as a whole consists
of four 'macro-variations'.

The first, treating the whole of Ex. 9 as an ostinato-pattern,
accumulates further elements around it. The music is filled with
small tapping and rustling sounds as piano, glockenspiel, cymbals,
triangle, tambourine and castanets join in. Cor anglais and clarinet
meanwhile play a new variant of figure *x*, while muted violas
answer with one of Ex. 6. In the second variation the passacaglia-
theme rises from D minor/major to E minor/major and the music

becomes full of clicks and rattles and trills and tintinabulations –
a sort of locusts' dance – as xylophone, harp, piano, high woodwind and pizzicato violins play broken demisemiquaver figuration
developed from the violin flurries of Ex. 9. Development of Ex. 6
continues in the cellos and as the passacaglia-theme begins to
move to a different key in every bar, the orchestration becomes
ever more complex, ever more riotous. The variation rises to a
swift climax for full orchestra on A flat, then breaks off while an
unaccompanied bassoon stutters out a broken version of the
theme. In the third, lightly-scored variation the theme itself
begins to fragment and change shape, while the woodwind
develop a tune introduced by solo oboe – apparently new, but in
fact another variant of Ex. 5:

By the last bar the passacaglia-theme has all but disappeared and
in the fourth and shortest variation it is scarcely recognizable.
This is an enraged outburst for full orchestra, *accelerando e apassion-
ato*, built out of a powerful, desperate-sounding fusion of Exx. 6
and 10 and ending the passacaglia in two shuddering *fff* chords.
A recitative-like phrase stabs upwards from cellos and basses,
twice; and then a drum-roll on F and a grand, deliberate descending even-crotchet scale (most prominent in the brass) leads into
C sharp minor/major and a *second* passacaglia.

After the hectic, whirlwind activity of Passacaglia I, Passacaglia
II is more meditative, attempting to think, rather than force, the
issues of the symphony through to a conclusion. It has a double
theme:

The bass (11*b*) is partly a simplified version of the first passacaglia-theme (9*a*), partly a further development of the descending-scale idea. The flute's counter-melody is a new variation of Ex. 6. But in addition to these themes Brian provides a 'tailpiece': two more active bars in quicker tempo for piano, harp and pizzicato strings. We find that between variations, this 'tailpiece' extends until it becomes a part of the variation process itself.

The first variation is austere and melancholy, presenting 11*b* on 2 oboes above sombre chords on muted horns, cellos and basses; but the 'tailpiece' expands to 4 bars, a scrap of tune and a bubble of arpeggios on piano, harp, glockenspiel, flute and pizzicato violins. The second variation is dark and stern, with trombones boldly varying the opening phrase of 11*a* against furious string tremolos and further developments of the theme in violins and cellos. Then the 'tailpiece' is further extended into an episode in its own right, a rippling stream of harp and piano figuration mingling with the cold high sounds of piccolo, flute, glockenspiel and tremolo *sul ponticello* violins. The third variation is more martial and violent, with fierce snorting muted-trumpet figures against sinewy semiquaver motion in the bass and propulsive side-drum rhythms, recalling the galloping Ex. 4. The fourth and shortest variation follows, in which 'tailpiece' and variation are fused: piano and pizzicato strings further develop their lively material against a threatening variation of 11*b* by trombones, tuba, and euphonium. This makes a grim cadence into the fifth and final variation, a brief but shattering climax like a wild cry of grief, leaving no hope of resolution of the conflict. The culmination is on D minor/major, a final mighty statement of both Ex. 11's lamenting themes, while the 'tailpiece's' semiquaver figures flicker above like tongues of flame, from high woodwind, glockenspiel, xylophone and piano. It reaches an agonized fortissimo peak on E flat and is then abruptly cut off.

Beneath a soft string chord, cellos and basses quietly hint at what might be the basic shape of the passacaglia-themes. Then full brass and woodwind, *ppp*, put down the bare-fifth chord on B flat from the symphony's opening. Against this, a quiet descending scale is heard once more in the harp. The bare-fifth passes, ambiguous but immovable, to muted strings, divided in 10 parts. The harp scale sounds again, but now it is more enigmatic, with a clashing C-flat in it. A cor anglais sings a single rising major third, B-flat to D: a ray of light, as if the ending might be in B flat major. But the bare-fifth sounds on, uncommitted. Then – remote, unchanged, as at the beginning, Ex. 1*b* arises on a single muted horn, climbing inexorably to its D flat (implying B flat minor) and with a very quiet, sinister, foreign dissonance beneath it on 3 muted trombones. The bare-fifth resounds on, unresolved, unresolving, to the last, and vanishes finally in a barely-audible gong-stroke. The end, like the beginning, is dark as night, and leaves the symphony stuck fast on the horns of its tragic dilemma.

11 Symphony No. 9 in A minor (1951)

1. *Adagio – Allegro Vivo*   2. *Adagio*   3. *Allegro Moderato*

Having completed Symphony No. 8, Brian proceeded to compose a full-scale, 3-act opera. The task occupied him until 1951. This was *Turandot, Prinzessin von China*, subtitled 'ein tragikomisches Märchen' and setting (in German) Schiller's version of Gozzi's fable. It has little in common with the Turandot operas of Puccini and Busoni, but it is one of Brian's most important scores: a crucial and fascinating work, in which all the features (those already developed and those yet to be explored) of his late style gell together in an artistic synthesis of exuberant power, colour and variety. The wild lyricism and militaristic violence of Symphony No. 8 both find their place in the fairy-tale world of ancient China, along with music of glittering ceremonial pageantry and moments of cool serenity (such as the beautiful nocturnal prelude to Act III), forming an imaginative unity that embraces high drama, comedy and a kind of stylistic parody (as in the Act II Minuet and the glumly Beethovenian funeral march in the final scene). The music is essentially symphonic and a full half-dozen orchestral episodes are worthy of concert performance. In many ways *Turandot* sets the tone for the music of Brian's final decades and its relative detachment and triumphant sense of artistic command must surely have helped him approach his complex, turbulent Ninth Symphony, which squarely confronts the tragic world of the Eighth and battles its way to victory.

Turandot was completed on 18 May, 1951 and by July the composer was hard at work on his new symphony. It was sketched by September and before the end of November the entire work had been completed in full score. (The sheer energy implied by such swift working is astonishing in a man of 75.) Symphony No. 9 is

in three movements played without a break and is dedicated to
the conductor Eric Warr who, the previous year, had given the
première performance of *The Tinker's Wedding* with the BBC
Scottish Orchestra. It is scored for forces roughly similar to No. 8:
there is no euphonium but Brian adds a 4th trumpet and bassoon
and the percussion department consists of timpani, organ, harp,
celesta, glockenspiel, xylophone, tubular bells, gong, triangle,
tambourine, cymbals, bass drum and 3 side drums. The work
lasts about 27 minutes.

Superficially the symphony follows a not unfamiliar course: a
dramatic, argumentative first movement, a slow, elegiac second
and a triumphant finale. At first glance, also, its structure is
traditional, for the outer movements are both sonata designs (the
only ones at this period in Brian's work) with a good deal of
literal recapitulation. But, as soon as we look more closely,
Brian's fundamental originality becomes apparent. The music of
the first movement is exceptionally tough and abrasive in character: it is concerned with struggle, and in its heroic wrestlings
Brian treats the conventional form with no more respect than in
The Gothic or Symphony No. 3.[1] Sonata-structure becomes a
'background', merely the framework for unconventional processes of his own. There is certainly thematic invention, but the
themes are less important than the kind of motion they engender;
there is masterly use of tonality, but tonal movement is never in
the direction we expect; the sense of struggle, of heroic effort and
involvement, is paramount.

The work begins with a forbidding, granitic introduction – a
static, leaden octave A, against whose immobility the bass instruments toil to initiate some motion (Ex. 1).

The orchestra stirs to life. A stern phrase from the brass leads
to a swelling crescendo in tremolo strings that seems to anticipate
a cadence into D and the start of the main movement. But the

---

[1] As the musical reader will have realized long before now, I am using 'sonata-
form' in its debased textbook sense of a primarily thematic structure – a misconception which does scant justice to the living tonal language of the real thing, as it
flourished in the work of Mozart, Haydn, and Beethoven. But it is a useful
misconception, insofar as it has been firmly established in the minds of listeners,
and indeed of many composers, since the mid-19th century. Brian's musical thought
reacts against it positively, and in his quest for free, dramatic, yet organic processes
he shows himself nearer to Beethoven in spirit than Czerny (Beethoven's pupil,
and the first man to define 'sonata-form') ever was.

tonal situation is not as clear as that. The opening bars have been *on* A, not *in* that key; and now follows music which soon develops leanings, not to D, but towards B flat. Tonal ambiguity is a hallmark of the first two movements; in the first, the doubt as to whether A (minor) is the main key or merely a persistently unresolved dominant contributes largely to the continual sense of effort and uncertainty – of the music, as it were, living by its wits in an unfriendly world. Nor is the structural position simple, for though the tempo now quickens, the music we hear

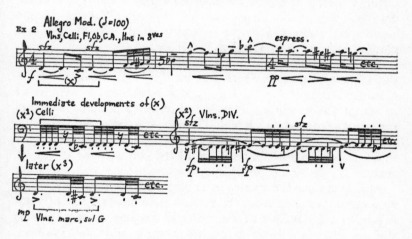

is in fact a transition-passage. But Ex. 2 (never to reappear) is a highly important theme: its first 3 notes (figure *x*) announce a fundamental idea. Unremarkable in itself, this figure is to travel right through the symphony in many different guises, imparting a far-reaching unity to its processes. In handling such a basic motive Brian shows an almost Brahmsian resourcefulness. As the transition continues and the music gathers way, *x* immediately begins to be developed on strings and horns, as shown (x^1, x^2) in the example. In the midst of these developments, with the tonal situation still unresolved, the pace reaches *Allegro Vivo* and the first subject appears in B flat minor (the Eighth Symphony's main key and the darkest so far).

It is not *as a theme* that Ex. 3 draws attention to itself. The listener is first aware of it primarily as a certain kind of motion – agile, wiry, combative – somehow suggestive of intellectual as well as physical toughness and flexibility. It is the perfect instrument through which to attack the problems presented by the intro-duction – the emotional problem of fighting a lowering tragic gloom and the technical one of maintaining onward pace and motion without tonal stability.

The first-subject group is essentially an accumulation of many short figures (especially developments of x in the brass) which are drawn into the orbit of the Ex. 3 theme by the tensile strength of its activity, as it continually coils and re-forms in different shapes that are later to be developed. The whole passage is marked by great nervous energy and tonal ambiguity, until near the end A minor is definitely established – followed (with a sense of emerg-ence, as if gaining a plateau) by A major.

Almost at once the music passes into the second subject, which I do not quote as its main theme proves to have no independent importance. It is a scrap of tune on a trilling oboe, accompanied by shifting chromatic patterns on low flute, clarinet and bassoon; this gives way to some beautiful (but harmonically tense) counter-point in the lower reaches of the orchestra. The melodic interest is in fact very slight, but melodic interest is not necessary – the breadth of the phrases and more consistent textures are all that Brian needs to furnish a breathing-space. The music moves into the region of E minor and then the turmoil resumes as it plunges into the development section.

Development begins with urgent reiterations of x on violas
with side-drum rhythmic assistance and a sweeping string phrase

whose final 4-note fragment (Ex. 4a), itself related to x, is immediately seized upon for powerful, obsessive motivic working. The
actual 'developmental' process here is oblique: 4a initiates a
rushing semiquaver motion which steadily powers the music for
the next few minutes, despite its strange and often fragmented
orchestration. This motion suggests a kinship with the first
subject even though Ex. 3 is not, as yet, directly alluded to –
another instance of the unity of Brian's music lying deeper than
mere thematic identity.

The music rushes on with weird orchestral sonorities: the
inevitable image is of a man fighting his way through jungle
undergrowth, his surroundings implacably hostile, but his courage
and will to resist undiminished. Once his progress is slowed: a
more direct reference to Ex. 3 in the strings and a massive rallentando for full brass lead to a few quiet, simple bars for strings and
woodwind, hinting at A minor in longer note-values: and we
realize that for all its tigerish energy this movement is very
broadly-paced and the furious semiquaver motion reflects only its
passionate intellectual struggle, not its unshakeable inner calm.

But the note-values diminish again and the sense of speed increases, leading to a great tutti upheaval based on developments
of 4a and the figure 1a from the introduction. Then a brief, hurry-
ing transition brings us to a doggedly striding passage that
reintroduces more elements from the introduction, especially the
variation of x shown in Ex. 2 as x^3. This is heard as a note of
warning on clarinets and side-drums, with counterpoints in low
woodwind and strings that stem from Ex. 1. The mood of fore-
boding deepens as muted trumpets, horns and gong enter the
texture. Then the air seems to clear, but x^3 is still tense when it is
heard in turn on solo bassoon, violins *sul G*, solo muted trumpet

and solo horn. The horn holds a sustained G and the music unexpectedly cadences into C major, where it finds a haven of stillness and deep tranquillity. For a moment at least, combat is forgotten, the key is firm, counterpoint nonexistent; there is only a beautiful horn solo, and the cellos' calm response:

Once again Brian has secured the maximum contrast and relief by single broad stroke; and the use of tonality here is a typical allusion, suggesting A minor only by association, through its relative C major. Yet the dogged, obstinate figure x^3 returns on low woodwind and the peace is disturbed by cloudy harmonies. Then a wild, tearing call for all 4 trumpets in unison lets loose the struggle again. The final span of the development, its material stormy and disruptive, soon runs its course and slows on a brief but majestic brass fanfare. The recapitulation swiftly ensues, *tempo comodo ma agitato.*

The recall of the first subject is almost exact, but the orchestration is completely reworked, the tonal setting is different and the few changes in details of the substance should not be overlooked. The whole passage is bodily transposed a tone higher, which has the effect of heightening its intensity (just as every detail in the changed orchestration adds greater bite and definition). The A major 'plateau' thus returns as a shining B major, its brightness enhanced by celesta chords at this point. So, despite its near-literalness in regard to substance, we are made to feel a *difference* in the recapitulation: the music of the exposition is shown to have attained, if not victory, then a kind of tough maturity.

The second subject, however, does not appear at all: it was always eminently dispensable and had no part in the development. Instead, a brief, halting, cadenza-like passage on solo clarinet allows the music to gather itself for the leap into a quick coda,

Vivace. This is based entirely on the music of Ex. 3 and with
swirling string figures and sharp trumpet-calls it rises swiftly to a
heroic, determined climax. At the height of its power there is a
sudden fermata and, in one of Brian's most uncanny inspirations,
the movement simply dissolves. Over a pedal F drum-roll,
supported by bass drum and suspended cymbal, all the energy
evanesces in a few scattered fragments: a harp glissando, murky
figures from horns and muted trombones, and a woodwind trill
that floats downward from piccolo through flute and clarinet to
bass clarinet, which leads the way into the slow movement.[1]

The central *Adagio* is essentially an elegiac movement, a serious
reflection where the first movement had been all muscular action:
tinged with the tragedy of things, but basically objective – more
like a funeral ode than a personal expression of sorrow. It is
intimately related to the preceding movement and it can be seen
to continue to explore issues already raised, bringing them to
some kind of conclusion. The threnodic main theme, announced
by solo cor anglais, touches on this complex skein of relationships:

In general contour it recalls Ex. 5 and there is a similar harmonic
ambiguity to that at the symphony's opening – the melody
suggesting A minor and the low string chords A major, with a
move towards B flat; and the cellos' continuation of the theme
shows that x is with us still, in a new guise.

The violins take up Ex. 6's first phrase against soft gong-
strokes; muted brass make more pointed references to x; and the

[1] The music here is strikingly similar to that which signals the melting of the
heroine's heart in the final scene of Brian's *Turandot*.

melody grows into a new, more impassioned theme, bringing with it some beautiful counterpoints on muted strings and trumpets. Woodwind and strings alternate in further developments, until the music moves into C minor and trombones and tubas quietly introduce a new stalking theme with a prominent dotted-note rhythm, which descends against tolling E-flats in the trumpets. Quietly, first the cellos, then other bass instruments, form a meandering line that makes more and more use of semiquaver figuration – so that, while there is little increase in tempo, the music begins to stir with calm and purposeful activity. The semiquavers float up through the strings until violins and solo flute share a long line which (though the notes are not the same) has the characteristic sinewy motion of Ex. 3 from the first movement.

The dotted-note theme begins to be developed on low woodwind against rising semiquaver arpeggios on a solo violin. Then 3 flutes hint once more at Ex. 3 while the cellos take over the dotted-note idea, which soon appears as a kind of fanfare in the woodwind:

The emotional temperature is increasing, and development of both ideas unleashes a powerful contrapuntal passage which ascends to the movement's first real climax. This is cut off abruptly and a final variation of the dotted-note idea – in D minor on all bass instruments including organ pedals – fades into the distance against a bass drum roll.

Ex. 6 now returns sadly on the cor anglais, again in A minor/ major, but its continuation on the strings is much changed. It moves to G flat, and then suddenly the figure x^3 from the first movement sounds anew, quietly and sinisterly on full strings and side-drum, and loudly, urgently, on the trumpets. This is the movement's crisis. A violent climax, based entirely on x^3, heaves itself up like some monstrous giant, never clearly recognized in the first movement, but now revealed and shaking its fist in fury. But it is impotent fury. The climax breaks off and dies, to the rhythm of x^3 on F-sharp, in solo timpani. Pianissimo, in C sharp, the first violins give out Ex. 6 against soft brass chords. Hesitantly at first, but with growing warmth, the music steers to a beautiful conclusion on strings alone, finally grounding in a calm, un-challenged A major. But not only does Brian at last confirm A as a key; he also provides the resolution of the 'unresolved dominant' feeling it has had throughout. For after the slow movement's last tranquil chord, the finale bursts out triumphantly – in D major.

Ex 8

The finale conveys triumph and fullness of heart, but not in any shallow way, for it continues the developmental processes of the preceding movements with tension as well as supercharged festive energy and climbs to one of Brian's most overwhelming con-clusions. Nor is the triumph conventionally expressed. Ex. 8, for instance, is a powerfully assertive statement, but one could not call it a *tune*: it is a highly-charged complex of short, individual ideas, whose brief phrases sum up the essence of a whole host of tunes and delineate by melodic gesture the nature of optimism and victory. (Note also that Ex. 8 carries with it figure x, its shape now reduced to a grace-note ictus that helps propel the music along.)

Formally the music has been seen as another sonata-design, but the identification is by no means exact. It is more like an enormous rondo in which a third and final return of the main subject is rejected in favour of a distantly-related coda which, as so often in Brian's music, has the effect of 'opening out' the form. In fact the 'exposition' initiated by Ex. 8 has no trace of clearly-defined first and second subjects. Instead, the whole vigorous span of music is built up, like Ex. 8 itself, by a continual accumulation of short, vigorous motives which Brian binds together with immense skill and brilliant orchestration (featuring much bold trumpet writing) to form a single pulsing torrent of exuberant symphonic energy. The 'grace-note' form of x proves a ubiquitous accompaniment figure and source of impetus. The motives themselves are many and varied: one of the most striking is an idea of colossal simple stateliness that Robert Simpson has likened to 'a titanic minuet' – though its spirit seems to me rather that of a very grand ceremonial march with humbler onlookers trying to keep in step:[1]

Shortly after this a *poco stringendo* passage leads straight into the 'development section', which is in fact much more a self-contained episode than in the first movement. It begins vivaciously in D minor, with canonic discussion of a new rather Elgarian theme of falling arpeggios and rising answering scales. But the tempo soon slows and the key changes to a majestic C minor, for a full orchestral climax (including organ pedals and bells), partially founded on the figure 8*a*. The music emerges from this turbulent but heady region and, slowing and quietening, moves towards one of the most affecting episodes in the entire work.

[1] Several prototypes for this idea may be found in *Turandot* where Brian first explored the use of a not-too-serious 'ceremonial' style.

Once again we find Brian hingeing a complex, massively-energetic movement around an episode of utter stillness and simplicity. The strings divide into 10 parts, in tranquil, uncomplicated harmony and pass among themselves a serene, gently-rocking figure while deep bells toll in remote, mysterious depths. It is very beautiful, nocturnal, almost dreamlike music. Who could imagine that this is simply another transformation of figure *x*?:

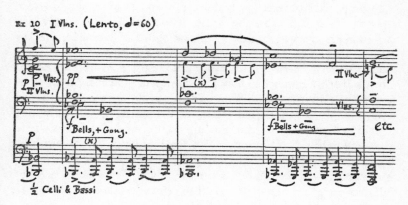

At length the episode dissolves in a tremolo crescendo and the 'recapitulation' bursts in. This is a verbatim repeat of the movement's opening statement, with no rescoring or new tonal setting: it would hardly be possible to make the original *more* exciting, more massively ebullient, than it already is. Also the literal repetition somehow accords well with the more formal and ceremonious aspects of the finale. It is when the repeat is over that the really interesting things happen. Brian takes the original *poco stringendo* transition and extends it into a second development, centred round figure 8*a*, while the music's gaiety and affirmation are reflected in ever more brilliant scoring. Eventually the great tide of invention slows and pauses expectantly on a grandiose chord of F sharp.

Then, with a solemn but glowing mass of orchestral polyphony, through which the trumpets shine forth proudly like the sun piercing storm-clouds, the coda begins. Its origins are in the earlier parts of the movement (especially Ex. 9), but as so often, Brian gives the impression of ending with something entirely new. The tempo has not slackened, but the pace is much broader, and brass chords, majestic series of figuration and powerful harmonic tensions pull in different directions, all over the orchestra, with the grandeur and exhilaration of the many motions on a stormy, yet sunlit sea. The sheer tumultuous splendour of the writing is breathtaking. No conventional triumph this: beside it many more celebrated symphonic apotheoses seem puny and half-hearted.

In time, after an immensely deliberate and weighty modulation, starting from B flat on the brass, has climaxed dazzlingly and quite unforeseeably in a full orchestral chord of E major, the key returns to D and solo timpani beat out a figure whose rhythm alone reminds us of x, the motive which has so influenced the work's stormy course. Horns and trumpets give tongue in a last sonorous, triumphant fanfare, and the symphony's accumulated energy explodes in a final eight victorious bars, full of strong dancing rhythms and the pealing clangour of tubular bells, glockenspiel and xylophone. The final cadence is the simplest dominant-tonic, from A to D major – the movement that was frustrated in the symphony's opening bars. Writ huge now by full orchestra and organ, it has all the thunderous conviction of a new discovery.

Symphony No. 10 in C minor
(1953–54)

The battling, heroic style of the Ninth Symphony is echoed in
Brian's next work, the opera *The Cenci*, which occupied him until
December 1952. This setting of Shelley's lurid Renaissance
tragedy opens with a long overture, very similar in spirit to the
Ninth's first movement, which could almost stand as a further
one-movement symphony.[1] The opera as a whole is one of
Brian's most highly-coloured creations: if Shelley's tale of incest
and murder makes a poor stage play, it is an excellent vehicle for
opera, and the music lends conviction to the melodrama, creating
a flaming, fast-moving theatrical spectacle. In the final scene,
however, there is an important development. The heroine
Beatrice, wronged by all and condemned to death with scant
justice, goes to the block resigned and calm; her last words –
'Well, 'tis very well' – are an expression both of personal integrity and of reconciliation to the inscrutability of fate. Brian's
music eloquently conveys this. It is perhaps the first occasion on
which that particular sense of stoic acceptance enters his music
and it is expressed even more strongly in his next symphony,
the Tenth.

That work was not to be completed for more than a year,
however. It seems as if Brian felt the need of a respite from deeply
serious music, for his next composition was a kind of 'holiday'
task, a collection of orchestral pieces in lighter vein entitled *Rustic
Scenes*, which he later numbered as *English Suite No. 5*. Completed
on June 27, 1953, it is maybe the most successful of all his essays
in a pastoral style that, ever since *Pantalon and Columbine* (1899),

[1] Brian in fact made a separate score of the piece for concert performance, giving
it the title *Preludio Tragico*.

Symphony No. 10: *the first pencil sketch of the 'storm'*

had celebrated a sturdy (and by now long-dead) rural life far removed from the nature-mysticism of Vaughan Williams or Holst. His attention was again diverted by the imminent BBC première of Symphony No. 8: he had to copy out the complete set of parts himself. That done, however, he started work on a new symphony and finished it on January 16, 1954.

Like Symphony No. 9, the Tenth again confronts the tragedy implicit in No. 8 with affirmative human activity. But its frame of reference is much wider than in the two preceding members of the 'trilogy': the music seems to measure the human spirit against the forces of Nature and, behind these, the still immensity of the Universe. In earlier symphonies we experience sudden moments of 'revelation', a 'widening of the horizons', that hints at some mysterious force in the background of the music. But in the Tenth the horizons are suddenly seen to be infinite, and human aspiration – however powerful – as something very small. The towering optimism of the Ninth's coda is no longer enough: something like the stoic heroism of Shelley's Beatrice is required. Brian's symphonies always voyage onward into new realms of experience and a deeper view of life. His is some of the least complacent music ever written.

Symphony No. 10 is scored for triple woodwind, strings, 4 horns, 4 trumpets, 3 trombones, euphonium, tuba, timpani, 2 harps, glockenspiel, xylophone, triangle, cymbals, bass drum, 3 side drums, thunder machine and – unique in Brian's *oeuvre* – wind machine: the last two instruments to some extent symbolize natural forces. Like the Eighth it is in one movement and like it also its processes of development are highly organic and unique to itself, although in this case there is a distant likeness to sonata structure. There is only one principal theme from which Brian's continuous working-out wrings the suggestion of a large-scale exposition, development and recapitulation; yet this is merged with an implied 'vestigial' 4-movement form comprising a moderately-paced first movement, a storm-like scherzo, a slow movement, and a march-like finale. But these clumsy terms have only limited usefulness and convey little of the subtle organism that is the symphony itself.

Brian's Tenth Symphony begins *Adagio e Solenne* with a noble, purposeful march-tune, approaching C minor through A flat, powerfully propelled by characteristic demisemiquaver ictuses:

These demisemiquaver groups form and re-form an absolutely basic, binding figure that, as in Symphony No. 9, is progressively developed throughout the entire work. Again we mark it *x*. By bar 3, side-drums are adding their martial impulse; at bar 5, the trumpets enter, varying *x*, and soon they swoop up to a high C-flat with thrilling effect. Plainly, we are setting out on some great endeavour. Yet this stern, resolute march-music has only just got under way when it is broken off, and, after a pause, there comes a complete change of character and texture.

By now we are familiar with the sudden interruptions and contrasts in Brian's symphonism. As well as providing variety of momentum they sometimes (as in Symphony No. 8) create dramatic oppositions; in other cases they often induce what one can only describe as a shift in *perspective*, in the way we view the music that has gone before. That is the case here. We are now confronted with a cold, rather unearthly sound: long high notes on solo flute, fragments of melody on solo oboe, quietly-tapping timpani, and a repeated muttering 4-note figure (based, like the oboe fragments, on *x*) on solo bassoon. The thin, wide-set textures create an effect of great vertical space. We have met this kind of episode before in other works, but its appearance in this one is unsettlingly early. The grand gesture of the opening is being placed right away in a chill perspective.

Greater warmth is infused as the orchestration grows fuller, fragments of the opening are recalled and the bass instruments urge greater activity. But after only a few bars the tempo slows to *Adagio* and a new melodic shape is heard high and lonely on flutes. Sombrely, euphonium, tuba and bassoons take it up, meditating on it for a moment before cadencing deliberately into F; and activity resumes, in the strings, with this theme:

Its opening phrase has grown out of the figure in the previous bars, but – although the effect is at first of something new – we see that it is in fact closely related to Ex. 1 and is indeed largely built out of figure *x*. Oboes take up the theme, and then the gallant trumpets from the start of the work re-enter, sounding once more a note of high endeavour.

Again the momentum is broken – but only for a few bars, until, *poco accel. e animato*, the music launches into a powerful discussion of Ex. 2. The forces of heroism are asserting themselves in full strength and a full-orchestral climax transforms Ex. 2 into a majestic slow march. Yet this climax lasts only 4 bars and a brief transition of cloudy harmonies and sinister orchestration initiates a long winding-down of momentum that will end the first section of the symphony in utter stillness.

First comes a calm colloquy among the strings, concerning the first bar of Ex. 2, which is soon reduced to the shape of figure *x*. Then the perspective begins to widen as the textures become lighter and more widely-spaced and new mournful figures sound in high woodwind and violins:

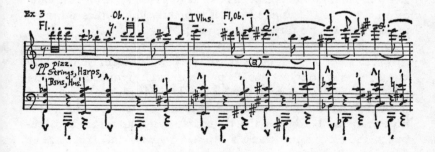

There is no real 'second subject' in the design of this symphony,

but Ex. 3 (which stems from descending brass figures at the very
opening and will be developed later) is the nearest approach to
one. It is not dwelt on, however. The textures continue to thin
out and warmth gradually recedes from the music throughout the
next short *semplice* section (distantly derived from Ex. 1); until,
suddenly, the music seems to step out into limitless space, in a
tranquil, wide-spaced pianissimo chord for horns and strings.

Of all Brian's 'points of stillness' – those areas of immobility
that lie at the heart of so many vigorous symphonic movements–
this is one of the most impressive. It seems to consist almost of
nothing and yet exercises an uncanny power. Against long-held
string chords comes a breath from muted horns, a slight movement in the cellos; basses, harps and glockenspiel, in turn, pick
out isolated notes; flute and piccolo shine in a high major second,
a beam of ghostly light. The effect in performance is magical; the
listener is conscious of enormous height and depth and distance,
of absolute, inhuman calm, as mysterious as that of the stars that
look down from a clear night sky.

Ex 4

Brian has shifted the perspective so as to give us the longest view
of all. Beyond the dogged heroism of his symphonies waits an
unanswerable, and unanswering, void.

Out of the vast quietness there arises a storm, *Allegro con fuoco*,
that serves the symphony as scherzo-section. 'Storm' is the only
word for it although it has no programmatic significance. It is a
mighty metaphor of an interior, psychological upheaval, expressed
in the imagery of nature. As such it is one of the great onomato-
poeic representations of the elements, standing somewhere between the storms in Strauss's *Alpine Symphony* and Beethoven's
Pastoral, although its individual character and intensity are
Brian's alone. It is almost impossible to describe except in natural-

istic terms, for apart from some development of x and the descending phrases (which can easily be missed in the tumult) the music is entirely athematic, making its impact largely through the orchestration which is among the most staggeringly imaginative (and virtuosic) Brian ever devised.

The wind and thunder machines are employed with comparative restraint: far more is demanded of whirling strings, skittering xylophone and bravely-plunging brass. Brian evokes, with unparalleled vividness, the myriad details of a howling gale, cracks of thunder, wicked flashes of lightning, viciously buffetting gusts of wind and rain falling in lashing sheets. It is truly malevolent weather and the music gives it almost physical impact. But there is no overstatement – its concentrated power lasts only a few minutes. Brian soon brings it to a climax in a great roar of bass drum, side drums, wind and thunder machines – and then suddenly (*tempo comodo*) all has vanished, except a pattering semiquaver violin figure, like the last few stray drops of rain.

A wispy pianissimo sextuplet ostinato now arises on divided violas – almost as if the ground were beginning to steam. Beneath these vapours solo woodwind, beginning with bassoon, start a kind of sinister fugato based on the first bar of Ex. 1. Bass clarinet, cellos, muted horns and cor anglais join in, but the insubstantial sextuplet figuration grows also, rising like a weird, swirling mist on violas and violins. The heavy brass enter with more descending phrases, and with a last roll of thunder the 'storm' blows itself out in E minor. A pause; and then, 'far away in the distance', an offstage trumpet-call is heard – solitary, yet proud. Unlike the trumpet-calls in the *Sinfonia Tragica* there is no mystery about it, but it is no less affecting than they. For the trumpet is a very human instrument and the sound of its bright tones at this juncture suggests that, despite the void and the hurricane, the individual spirit still survives and, alone in the storm-drenched landscape, greets the return of the sun.

Mysterious tramping figures in the woodwind, supported by pizzicato strings and further developing the descending phrases, lead us to a section marked *Lento espressivo*, which does duty as a slow movement by providing much-needed lyrical relief. A solo oboe, accompanied by cellos divided in four parts, steers into C major; and then a solo violin takes up the oboe phrases and expands them into a melody of simple, singing beauty:

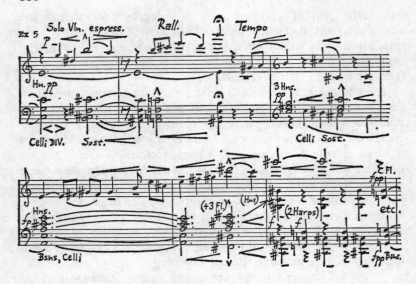

Ex 5

Throughout this section the violin dominates, very much in the spirit of Ex. 5, but developing continuously and organically from that preliminary statement, in some of Brian's most eloquently beautiful music. As with the trumpet fanfare, the solo instrument seems in some sense a symbol of individual humanity, the tender phrases affirming the worth of personal emotion against the vastness of space. At first the other instruments merely accompany the soloist, but then a bold, fanfare-like motive on brass and percussion propels the music towards a peak in which the full power of the orchestra is heard: a passage of mounting intensity, based on chromatically-descending figures that originate in those of Ex. 3 (especially 3a). Above this the violin sings passionately in its highest register. At last comes a great climax; a rhetorical *ritardando*, as the violin sails up to a high A; and then, *più vivo*, the 'finale' section of the symphony breaks out with fierce, dogged march-rhythms in A major.

This 'finale' answers, balances, and fulfils the march-like gesture with which the work opened, and it is based on the same material. But after the experience of the intervening episodes, its character is very different. The mood is grimly triumphant, but also tough and hard-bitten; the rhythms are irregular, the orchestration is strangely fragmented and the march carries along with it some memories of the violence and fury of the 'storm'. But it is enormously affirmative and soon the trumpets lift up brazen voices in a proclamation of defiant, savage joy that glorifies Ex. 1 and Ex. 2 in the same phrase:

Onward strides the stark march, sometimes mighty and towering as in Ex. 6, sometimes gathering around itself jagged fragments of Exx. 1 and 2, splintered up across the whole range of the orchestra. However spasmodic these fragments may be, Brian binds them together and maintains the driving forward momentum with absolute certainty of purpose. Eventually the march culminates in a massive upheaval for full orchestra, including wind and thunder machines; characteristically it is abruptly cut off, on a vehement unison C.

There follows one of Brian's strangest and most wonderful codas, which not only qualifies the triumphal ferocity of the 'march, but is also, in a sense, the conclusion that the Eighth, Ninth and Tenth Symphonies have all been seeking. Muted, divided cellos, violas, violins and woodwind twice build up, softly, stepwise, a mass of peaceful suspended harmony, concluding on G. Between these masses the violas gently oscillate in what might be the basic shape of x, on C. Solo woodwind, uncertain, try to suggest a final key: cor anglais and clarinet think it might be F sharp; bassoons and contra-bassoon say the exact opposite – C major. Then, without warning, an astonishing, enigmatic pianissimo chord stares at us, sphinx-like and inscrutable, from full brass. It could be the dominant of C flat, but its identity is obscured by added notes and wide spacing and somewhere within it a drum softly sounds a repeated B-flat. It hangs there, athwart the music, utterly static and mysterious. So might some gigantic supernova shine out of the depths of space, a cold, far-off, incomprehensible radiance, yet signifying the deaths of stars and worlds.

The baleful light vanishes into a shivering tremolo chord on G flat in *ponticello* strings and a barely audible drum-roll. Over this the solo violin, *espressivo*, is heard for the last time, singing the opening phrases of Ex. 5 against the darkness. It is a last poignant assertion of human integrity, but it also implies reconciliation: the universe is vast and mysterious; peace of mind lies only in a stoic, unafraid acceptance of the fact that there will be no answers . . . . 'Well, 'tis very well'. The final two quiet bars, ending the symphony not in C flat but in an unshakeable C *natural* major with a last, tranquil, slow-wheeling augmentation of figure *x*, have all the deep majesty of the distant night sky, and the calm of the stars in their courses.

13 Symphony No. 11 (1954)

1. *Adagio*   2. *Allegro giocoso*
3. *Maestoso e pesante – Allegro Marcia*

Brian's capacity for continued creative work at a rate that might have knocked out a man half his age seemed merely to increase as he grew older. Only a few weeks after bringing Symphony No. 10 to a close (and only a few days after his 78th birthday) he began his Eleventh, and sketched out the entire work in short score in the space of six days – this in spite of the fact that the new work, in three movements, was much longer than the Tenth. Indeed, the sketches show that much the biggest movement, the second, was conceived from beginning to end in a single day, February 11. The finale was drawn up by February 15 and the full score was completed on April 29, 1954.

Symphony No. 11 seems at first glance to stand apart from the main stream of Brian's creative concerns. The struggles and searchings of the preceding symphonies have no place in it. Instead, the first movement is the most tranquil music he ever wrote; the second is an expansive, incalculable, many-sided creation, neither scherzo nor slow movement, which plays hide-and-seek with all the listener's expectations; and the third is a brief, downright, massively optimistic march-like finale. It must be remembered that in a few months' time Brian was to begin writing the largest of all his late works, the opera *Faust*. Goethe's masterpiece had been a lifelong source of inspiration (in *The Gothic*, for instance) and by the time he completed Symphony No. 10 he must surely have known that, if he was spared a little longer, he would essay an opera on that text. It may be that he did not feel entirely ready for the attempt and wished for another respite from work on the high tragic plane. Thus Symphony No. 11 can be seen as another 'holiday' task – but of a far more subtle and sophisticated kind than *Rustic Scenes*.

For tranquillity of spirit does not preclude profundity of thought. On closer acquaintance Symphony No. 11 proves to follow No. 10 in more than just numerical sequence. The Tenth, we recall, ended with a kind of stoic calm, suggesting an acceptance of everything inscrutable and unknowable in life. The Eleventh *begins* with music of a very similar kind, which grows into a great, unruffled *Adagio*, as if this initial acceptance has brought complete serenity, the unshakeable quietude of a mind wholly at peace with the world. The later movements can then be seen as explorations of different aspects of that serenity (the playful and the optimistic) and the whole symphony as basically contemplative.

The work is scored for triple woodwind, brass including euphonium, strings, timpani, 2 harps, glockenspiel, xylophone, celesta, bass drum, 3 side drums, cymbals, tambourine, triangle, sleigh bells, and gong. On the title-page the composer has written: 'Basis of inspiration – Two Mottoes'; and the 'mottoes' – a phrase and its answer – follow:

It is one of the drolleries of the symphony that these 'mottoes' only take that shape in the second movement, and even then, *never* at that particular pitch. It seems as if Brian is giving us here the original melodic germ by which the symphony took root in his mind, at the pitch which first occurred to him. But such a basic shape can inform a symphonic work in many ways and it is with a foreshortened and rhythmically altered version of the 'mottoes' that the first movement begins – a gentle descending figure, around whose thread a fine-spun web of serene polyphony begins to form (Ex. 2).

Brian never wrote a less describable movement: like all of the simplest and deepest things in music, it crumbles to dust at the touch of a pen. It lasts about 10 minutes, yet the writer cannot trace its course by reference to events – it is wholly uneventful, and that is one of its essential qualities. Except in the final bars, the slow, floating, even-crotchet pulse never varies, nor the un-

troubled ebb and flow of the polyphony. Ex. 2 is merely the beginning of a vast, drifting motion in which there is no repetition, no hint of any recognizable form, but an absolute unity of feeling. The music is infused with a kind of cataleptic calm, even a kind of monotony – but it is the monotony of a vast still lake, or a completely cloudless sky – a monotony which is a function of scale and mystery.

The harmony, too, is un-dynamic, avoiding any high level of dissonance. But lesser levels are there and Brian's unobtrusive and masterly disposition of them throughout the contrapuntal fabric gives the music its life: the slight tensions and their resolutions suggest latent power beneath the surface, like the flexing of powerful muscles in a deep, untroubled sleep. The orchestration has an overall silver-grey quality that is unique in Brian's work; yet it is continually changing texture as the focus subtly shifts, bringing into prominence now strings, now low woodwind, now horns; here a cor anglais, there a pair of bassoons, elsewhere a solo violin. Though the whole effect is of quietude, the music does rise twice to short-lived fortissimo peaks (both in D major). They are not climaxes for they are as calm as anything in the movement. The second fortissimo swings, by a broad and majestic modulation, in the direction of F major; and shortly afterwards the movement concludes in that key on violins and harp, with a slow repeated F on the flutes.

Immediately, the next movement follows. The flutes' repeated F becomes a much faster crotchet-beat in 4/2 time, with harps, sleigh bells, tambourine, triangle, bass drum, suspended cymbal and pizzicato strings (rather reminiscent of the 'farmyard' sounds that open Mahler's Fourth Symphony). Against this background, the horns launch into a long and jovial tune in B flat:

Ex 3 Allegro giocoso ($\downarrow$=100)

Clearly, we are in for a good old-fashioned 'tuneful' scherzo, and the listener mentally settles down to enjoy something clear-cut and straightforward. That is always a mistake with Brian, whether he is in serious or humorous mood. Critics lacking familiarity with his mature idiom have sometimes unjustly accused Brian's music of being disjointed and directionless. The second movement of Symphony No. 11, however, might have been written especially to tease such critics. Interruptions and changes of direction are very much part of its humorous strategy: the listener's expectations are always being frustrated and gently mocked. The composer is not being merely self-indulgent. To avoid the expected at every turn is as good a structural principle as any and the movement is in fact very subtly organized, though in overall character it is best viewed as a series of variations, on a mood rather than a theme. Long before the end Brian has transformed it from a scherzo into a slow movement, though how he does it seems at first a baffling mystery. Music such as this seems designed to teach the unwary listener a lesson in patience: and that, after all, is an aspect of serenity.

A foretaste of future interruptions appears as soon as the horns have stated the opening tune. The tempo slows and, still in B flat, we hear a *Maestoso* interchange between upper and lower woodwind and strings on a ponderously square-cut version of the 'mottoes' (which, of course, also begin Ex. 3). The slower pace and rhythmic regularity of this development effectively disrupts the initial momentum; yet the passage climaxes with a rhetorical pause on a chord of D, muted trumpets perkily state the 'mottoes' at the original tempo and the scherzo-like music returns, this time in E flat. Ex. 3 is restated completely, chiefly in the strings, and the whole orchestra then proceeds to develop the material with all proper jollity and good humour. Very soon, however, the music's progress is unexpectedly brought up short by a rather plaintive figure:

The interval of a falling octave, already introduced by the low brass in the preceding bars, is to become an important unifying element in later developments. The scherzo music resumes again, but more tentatively now: it begins in C major but rapidly loses tonal stability – its 'tuneful' characteristics begin to disappear and soon another version of Ex. 4 brings it firmly to a close. The cellos lead straight into 'something entirely different'.

A curious little episode begins *molto meno mosso* with repeated harp chords, pizzicato falling octaves in cellos, a rather lachrymose oboe tune and a hiccupping accompaniment from a slightly bibulous bassoon. But there is more to come. A solo flute takes over the oboe melody and turns it into a kind of frail minuet – it acquires an air of gentle formality, of almost 'courtly' hauteur. Can this, we wonder, as the tune's phrases seem to nod and bow to one another – can this be Brian, the strong, heroic symphonist? Yes, it can, when he is in holiday mood – we are not meant to take the tune at its face value. Look at the accompaniment: while the flute tune preens itself on its good manners, the bassoons quietly mock it, plodding along behind in rustic, droning open fifths. This mating of the genteel and the homely is a ripe example of Brian's musical humour and also contributes to the music's air of faint unreality (Ex. 5).

The episode continues for a little, with cellos and basses softly introducing elements of Ex. 3 into the latter stages; and then, with some exquisite modulations (and variation of Ex. 4), it sinks into

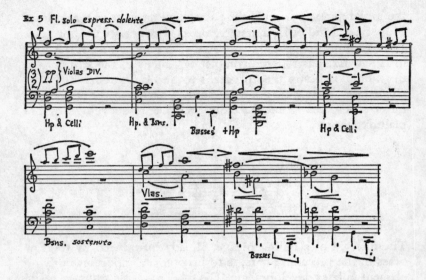

the pleasant backwater of a slumberous *Adagio*. What matter, Brian seems to be saying, if the music isn't getting anywhere? In this symphony there are no goals to aim at, no trials to be overcome, so why not enjoy the view?

The 'view' is certainly enchanting. The *Adagio* is full of long-breathed, polyphonic lines and lushly chromatic resultant harmony, made all the warmer by the richness of the orchestration. The lines are free, fantasia-like, yet Ex. 4 and elements of Ex. 3 continue to be metamorphosed throughout. The slow tempo persists until the possibility of a return to scherzo-like momentum seems to have vanished entirely. A bridge passage (scored principally for brass, harp, glockenspiel and xylophone), recalling the 'square-cut' variation of the 'mottoes' heard near the beginning of the movement, leads to a new self-contained episode that is as odd as the last. Against thrummed harp chords, oboe and bassoon sing a doleful little melody, which the strings punctuate now and then with solemn 'Amen'-like phrases, as shown in Ex. 6. It is pleasantly simple stuff and in a more orthodox movement by a less incalculable composer we would probably find it a little platitudinous. But like the 'minuet', it has an air of whimsical unreality. Still it takes itself quite seriously and goes on in similar vein for some time – long enough for a suspicion to form that it

is seriously meant. Only then does Brian upbraid our gullibility: with a jolt, the music returns in raucous good humour to scherzo-style – which we had never expected to hear again. Yet here it is, *Allegro giocoso*, with brass and percussion making a merry noise. The material is a much-varied and foreshortened form of Ex. 3, with a prominent dotted rhythm and much use of the 'mottoes' in diminution.

This outburst initiates some vigorous development, rather Haydnesque in spirit if not in style, centering around the new dotted rhythm, which soon acquires a definitive motivic shape that also proclaims kinship with the ubiquitous 'mottoes':

In due course Ex. 7 is reduced to an ostinato on flute and bassoon, accompanying muted horns. But excitement seems ready to flare up again; there is a crescendo, with a Wagnerian growl from euphonium and tuba – and yet another of Brian's sleight-of-hand changes. All is suddenly slow and tranquil again, as high wood-wind and harp gently vary the basic 'motto' shapes, expanding in an expressive vein with delicate scoring that is reminiscent of the quiescent first movement. The motion slows still further, bringing a lyrical horn solo. Tuba, cellos and basses make a calm, even-crotchet ostinato out of the 'mottoes'; then xylophone and glock-enspiel chime against brass chords in another variation of them.

There is a pause, and then, *Andante espress. teneramente*, there is an absolutely clear reference back to the first movement on full strings, in a rapt, warm F sharp major (the basic form of the 'mottoes' is to be found here too, unobtrusively, on the harps). From this benedictory descending phrase grows the movement's culminating section – four pages of serene, utterly beautiful music that rises to no climax but drifts slowly, on long-spanned string phrases, through some wonderful harmonies. It is possible to find almost all the previous material recalled in these pages, everything expressed now in the one untroubled even-crotchet 6/4 pulse, and numerous adaptations of the 'mottoes' also, in inversion and retrograde inversion. But it is better simply to enjoy it: the thematic coherence is there, but is intended to be felt, not noticed.

Almost imperceptibly, the warm *Andante* tails off into a lazy coda. The long-spanned string phrases, ultimately stemming from the 'mottoes', still curve contentedly up and down, but in sparer textures, while flutes, harp, glockenspiel and celesta lap against them with variants of Ex. 4. The use of the celesta at this point (its only appearance in the symphony) is a perfectly-judged detail of scoring, for its silvery, musical-box quality enhances the music's fragile delicacy as this long movement finally passes away. Gradually it seems to dissolve before our ears, until no motion is left, only a long-held string chord of G. But even now Brian is in no hurry. The chord continues, and, very softly, the sleigh-bells tap away at the original even-crotchet rhythm, which at this slow tempo has an almost dreamlike quality. Muted trumpets, pianissimo, hold on to the G chord; and cellos and basses quietly and finally state the 'mottoes' in their basic Ex. 1 form, concluding on a low G. Thus the movement fades into nothingness.

If the listener has found the course somewhat baffling and suspected that he was being made fun of, Brian now makes handsome amends with an admirably clear-cut, confident, tuneful finale, firmly in his most optimistic E major. 'Really more like a coda' was how Robert Simpson once described it; but brief though it is, it is a fully worked-out structure and there is nothing small about its mode of utterance. In fact it closely follows the ground-plan of the Ninth Symphony's finale (that is, a modified rondo, consisting of statement, episode, counterstatement passing into development-episode and coda), though on a much smaller scale and with much simpler material.

After a sturdy preliminary E major fanfare for brass and percussion (on a figure reminiscent of the opening of Haydn's *London* and Schubert's Second Symphony), woodwind and strings launch into the main finale-theme – a bluff, downright and immediately likeable march-tune:

Nothing could be more straightforward, and like many other Brian themes, it surely stems ultimately from the brass-band music he heard as a child. Yet a simple touch – the sudden, characteristic shift to C major at the fifth bar – serves to lift the tune above any hint of banality. Brian uses material of such popular appeal not, like Mahler, to parody it, but to transfigure it.

Ex. 8 is the beginning of a large, ebullient paragraph of related ideas, which are reviewed with much good humour in appropriately bright orchestration. Then the music slows and soon we come upon the main episode, a kind of rustic dance:

It starts from Ex. 9 – note that this too moves from E major to C – and from these first measures soars off into clear sunlit textures with an effortless flow of graceful, singing melody – light, relaxed, and yet with a hint of muscular power held in reserve. It is a rare reminder of the 'pastoral' style Brian tended to reserve for his lighter works – a style as fresh and English as Vaughan Williams's, though very different; and which he could express (as here) with unexpected polish and elegance. So wholly delicious is the episode that I refrain with difficulty from quoting its full 40 bars.

At the close, the Ex. 9 key-change is reversed and the episode modulates from C major back to E. Whereupon the *Allegro*

Marcia breaks out again with Ex. 8. The theme is restated exactly as before, and so is much of the continuation: but Brian does not bother to complete it, and breaks off instead for an extraordinary little piece of development. Horns, trumpets, euphonium and tuba start to blare out a 5-note figure (derived from 8*a*) in a series of dissonant, fanfare-like canonic entries. It is heard again and again; the tempo increases; the entries occur closer and closer together in a wild, invigorating stretto until the passage sweeps up into a broad, *Marcia Maestoso* version of Ex. 8's opening bars, for full orchestra. This grand statement, followed by a more solemn brass and percussion fanfare, initiates the coda, which refers no more to the main finale subject, except in its similarly optimistic character. The whole orchestra, with grandiloquent brass, strides purposefully towards a majestic resolution that was never really in doubt. For all the difference in expression, this coda enshrines the same simple yet deep serenity with which the work began. Just before the end, trumpets and trombones make a covert allusion to the 'mottoes'; then all is swallowed up in a blaze of E major glory.

14   Symphony No. 12 (1957)

The Eleventh Symphony was followed by a symphonic poem: at least, that is how Brian designated it, though no programme is apparent. *Elegy* (originally entitled *A Song of Sorrow*) was completed in June 1954 – a profound, gripping work whose stormy passages and great inward calm relate it both to Symphony No. 10 and the first movement of No. 11, although it has a strongly defined character of its own. In fact it could plausibly be described as a kind of Faustian character-study, comparable in this respect to Brahms's *Tragic Overture*; a last preparation for the great task that lay ahead. For Brian now embarked on *Faust* itself, a 4-act opera on Part I of Goethe's drama. It cannot be discussed here, except to remark that this peak of Brian's operatic output clearly represents the consummation towards which all his music had been moving since Symphony No. 8. It is a rather austere work, quite unlike any other composer's treatment of the theme, which will take plenty of getting to know in performance, let alone in score. But it also contains some of his most awe-inspiring music, for instance in the purely orchestral scene *Nacht: Offen Feld* that depicts the 'wild ride' of Faust and Mephistopheles.

Brian completed *Faust* in May 1956. He was over 80 years old and had successfully faced what was, for him, the ultimate challenge in musical composition. He wrote nothing for the next seven months: the longest pause since he had begun the *Sinfonia Tragica* nine years before. But since he remained hale and at the height of his creative powers, there was no reason for this to be the end. Throughout his life Brian considered himself at the mercy of musical impulses which came unwanted and unbidden and could not be denied. 'Something would start going through his head', and would give him no peace until he had got it down on paper. At the beginning of 1957 his head began to fill with music once more. He had been reading the *Agamemnon* of Aeschylus and this seems to have provided the initial stimulus for a new and strikingly original symphony, a work which might be said to embody the very *idea* of tragedy in its most solemn, exalted, and terrifying terms.

The Twelfth Symphony is scored for quite a large orchestra (triple woodwind, brass including 6 horns and euphonium, strings, timpani, harp, glockenspiel, xylophone, triangle, tambourine, castanets, cymbals, 3 side drums, bass drum and gong) but is the shortest Brian had yet written – a single-movement work lasting under 13 minutes. Such brevity is the product of extreme compression, not just in length but in argument, language and structure; and in saying that we should remember Schoenberg's dictum that 'compression is expansion'. What he renounces in duration Brian gains in power of suggestion: the work has all the impact of a 40-minute symphony. No wonder that, although one of his most immediately impressive creations, Symphony No. 12 is at first so difficult to comprehend. Within its single movement, four short sections may be discerned: an introduction and *Allegro moderato* corresponding to a first movement, a weighty funeral march, an intensely lyrical 'slow movement' for strings alone and an *Allegro vivo* 'finale' with a tiny epilogue.

Compression and suggestion are two of the work's salient characteristics – the third is great freedom of form. Thematic development in the strict sense has a much smaller function here than in the previous few symphonies; Brian is far more concerned to create unity out of diversity by balancing similar *types* of texture and activity and to establish links by allusion rather than restatement. Such procedures were foreshadowed by Part II of *The Gothic* and in *Das Siegeslied*, and had influenced his symphonic thought ever since. But he had never before applied them so sweepingly to a purely orchestral work. Without the controlling factor of a text, brevity was essential to prevent their getting out of hand; but equally such far-ranging, non-recapitulating music implies a longer-than-normal reach of thought and it is this which gives the symphony its sense of scale. Moreover, the most elusive music is in the outer sections: these are counterweighted by the funeral march, which is essentially a strict development of a single

rhythmic figure – one of the most rigorous and impressively
sustained pieces of invention, for its size, in Brian's entire output.
Such is his command of suggestion that the march (itself only 4
minutes of music) seems to dominate the whole work; in retrospect the other sections appear mere annexes to its huge, crushing,
doom-laden cortège, as though the symphony was the embodi-
ment of the chorus's cry in Aeschylus's *The Libation Bearers* –
'Where is the end? Where shall the fury of fate be stilled to sleep,
be done with?'

The Twelfth Symphony has one of the most imaginative
openings of them all. A high sustained A harmonic in the violins,
a low A timpani-roll, and in the cavernous space thus suggested,
bright, enigmatic glockenspiel notes – perhaps standing for the
stars, 'high-swung in ether, that bring men summer and winter',
spoken of by the Watchman in the first lines of the *Agamemnon*.
The tonality is apparently a kind of A; the symphony has in fact
no main key, but A (minor) is the centre towards which its fluid
activity most often inclines. Abruptly, even starlight is extin-
guished – there is the barest hint of a march-rhythm in the
timpani and strange shapes dart out from woodwind and muted
brass:

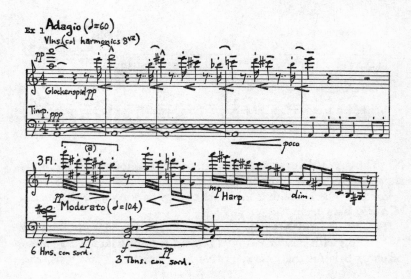

It is worth remarking that none of the symphonies I have so far
discussed has begun in a way even faintly similar to any of the
others. Even when the openings can be broadly classed together
by type (as 'march-like', for instance, in Nos. 3, 4, 8 and 10) each
has its own completely different character and atmosphere. Brian
seemingly had an inexhaustible ability to produce symphonic
'opening gambits' that proclaim from the outset both his own
unmistakable personality and the utter uniqueness of each
particular work.

The harp scale that concludes Ex. 1 descends to a slithering,
sinewy cello melody accompanied by low bassoons and trombones; then to a *rising* harp scale. None of the material heard so
far is to return – this is an oblique kind of introduction, outlining
certain *types* of motions and figures that will be encountered later.
Now high violins tensely state a figure in Brian's favourite
'funereal' rhythm, and it is soon taken up by violas (ex. 2a). It is
little different from the figure *x* that had such far-reaching conse-
quences in Symphony No. 9, so again *x* is how we label it. But
Brian's use of it in this work is less thoroughgoing than in the
earlier symphony: he is less interested in its melodic shape than
in the rhythm itself – this is the seed from which the funeral
march will grow. The violins follow 2a with a short rising melody
(2b), which *is* developed later, though very freely.

Note how swiftly everything is happening, although the tempo is
slow: Brian is creating a complex frame of reference for later
events, rapidly sketching in a host of associations with fragments
of a few bars each.

The music launches into a tough, hard-bitten *Allegro Moderato*
(beginning with Ex. 3a, below). The determining factor here as so
often in Brian is the bass line: this he extends and develops, and

it is its steely strength which really carries the weight of the argument onward. Ex. 3*a* soon grows into a powerfully energetic contrapuntal fantasy, involving the full orchestra for the first time. Figure *x* returns on high woodwind and percussion, some shards of the 2*b* melody are developed and a new, thrusting idea of repeated semiquavers appears and spreads through the orchestral fabric. But the bass is the real propulsive element, particularly its rising scale figure (Ex. 3*a*, second bar) which Brian develops urgently (it relates back to the harp scales of the opening). Soon Brian is able to sweep this complex of ideas to the work's first short, sharp, grim climax: which, in A minor and stemming from the repeated-note figure, is reminiscent of the battering motive *y* from the first movement of *The Gothic*.

The climax fades out towards E flat with a sombre variation of the first phrase of 2*b* in augmentation in the bass and a few bars of darkly expressive cor anglais solo. Then the *Allegro Moderato* returns (Ex. 3*b*).

That is, the *tempo* returns and there is a consequent sense of recapitulation as if we were in a tiny sonata-movement. But look at Exx. 3*a* and 3*b*! They begin on the same note and with nearly the same rhythm – but otherwise the passages are quite unrelated: the second cannot be considered a 'development', however distant, of the first. Nevertheless they have certain features in common: similarities of mood, scoring, rhythmic activity and direction. And it is out of these – by setting up, as it were, a complex of allusions – that Brian is able to impart a sense of real structural patterning and balance.

This 'recapitulation', if such it is, is short-lived. The music reaches A flat and a shadow suddenly falls. Slow, deliberate, inexorable, the principal motive of the funeral march creeps in quietly in the bass: a sound to put the fear of death into any listener, like the motion of Fate itself.

The sad violin melody above it is freely derived from Ex. 2*b*, but it is the bass rhythm (one of Brian's fingerprints, as we know) out of which the march is to be built. This becomes clear as soon as the full orchestra is unleashed in an enormous, rock-like tutti. Melodic fragments from other sources may weave in and out on woodwind and pitched percussion, but it is that rhythm (made convulsive by the strange orchestration – in which the last 2 demisemiquavers of each beat are hammered out by 6 horns, 3 side drums and castanets) which forms the music's bone, muscle and sinew. Its very deliberateness of pace is frightening. As the rhythm is repeated over and over again, time seems somehow expanded – every semiquaver rest becomes a yawning gap, the wait for the next thudding demisemiquaver group an age of almost unbearable tension.

Such unremitting stress cannot be long sustained. The music reaches A minor and Brian provides some relief by introducing more purely melodic writing in a less oppressive texture of solo woodwind and strings. Nevertheless, the melodic figures that now float up and down on clarinet, cor anglais, bass clarinet and violins stem directly from the march-rhythm; and that, too, is present, simply *as* a rhythm – soft, insistent, inescapable – on cellos and basses.

The tonality rises gradually to B flat major and for a moment the rhythm disappears while timpani establish a 4-note even-crotchet ostinato, over which the horns play calm, pacificatory chords. But the rhythm soon starts to insinuate itself again – first on flute and piccolo, who vary its off-beat demisemiquaver element with little 3- and 4-note flourishes: a bird-like sound, apt for some buzzard hovering far above doomed Mycenae. As the timpani ostinato continues, the music moves into C minor with a sorrowful flute theme, using the march-rhythm and directly related in shape to the bass of Ex. 4. Then two mighty chords for full orchestra initiate the march's final stage. Ex. 4's bass figure strives upwards, against *sforzando* chords, against the timpani ostinato, against muted-trumpet dissonance, on euphonium and

bassoons, with side-drum support. Out of its dogged effort, out of the enormous tension that has been gradually built up by this vast, unfeeling, irresistible momentum, there arises an over-whelming climax. Its stark power, heard in context, is indescrib-able. Ex. 5, above, cannot show the context, but it shows the thing itself. Pity and terror are here indeed; and when the music culminates in the great upward sweep of Ex. 5's last 2 bars, there is a tremendous sense of release, a true catharsis, wringing emotion dry.

The climax is prolonged for a further bar and a half. Then it vanishes and assuagement is brought by the cool, poised beauty of a 'slow movement'. Ex. 6, below, is its beginning. This symphony, unlike some that we have discussed, does not lead us through the *experience* of tragedy. The funeral march is more symbolic, embodying the essence of tragic feeling; and Brian is able to show us, behind this, a peace and serenity that remains undisturbed.

Though this 'movement' is a mere 23 bars in length, it falls into three distinct spans. The first, beginning from Ex. 6, broadens into warm, peaceful, spacious modulations that are quite different from anything we have heard so far. (And it is worth repeating that such extreme contrasts in such a short musical space have the effect of broadening the whole work, making it seem much larger than it is in mere durational time.) The second (*Lento*) span freely develops the lines of the first with a tender melody in first violins; while a counterpoint in second violins seems to the analyst's eye a distant relative of 2b. In the third span, which grows naturally out of the second, the tempo quickens and the harmony admits of the parallel-fifth and -fourth chords that were a characteristic of the funeral march. It ends in E flat and there is a short linking-passage on A, chiefly consisting of a long-held bassoon chord and distant muted horn-calls. Then the 'finale' breaks out, *Allegro vivo*.

This is shorter (in time) even than the 'slow movement', though of course much more eventful. It balances the previous *Allegro moderato* and relates to it in a general way. Apart from a very basic figure like *x*, nothing recurs exactly, but almost every event in the earlier section can be paralleled here by a similar kind of shape, activity or texture. So, as in the *Allegro moderato* itself (at 3*b*) we find something like 'recapitulation by allusion'. However, this section also introduces new elements – the only really 'light' ones in the symphony. It begins boldly and heroically with the brass, especially trumpets, much in evidence, and plenty of strong rhythmic interest. But before long a sort of grotesque humour has invaded the music – nowhere more strongly than where a trombone has a boisterous solo against a skittering semiquaver accompaniment of xylophone and piccolo. Although this might seem inappropriate to the deep seriousness that has gone before, I personally find it a necessary and just reaction to the awesome gloom of the funeral march. After all, Greek tragic trilogies were usually rounded off by a comic satyr-play, a celebration of continuing life.

Eventually, after some tumultuous orchestral invention that makes a real field-day for the percussion, the music touches A minor and there slows, suddenly becoming invested with stormy grandeur. A terse figure recalling 1*a* from the introduction (though not exactly, of course – this is another 'allusion') is proclaimed by the trumpets and taken up by low brass. The tempo becomes *Adagio ma pesante*; all bass instruments growl out a totally new theme (unless it is an 'allusion' to the cello theme of the opening); and there is a sudden violent, shuddering climax, abruptly cut off.

There is a pause, and then the symphony concludes with three very simple bars of coda. Horns, violins and violas hold a *ppp* sustained bare-fifth chord on C, while cellos, basses and timpani reiterate a minor-third shape, C-A-C, in a rhythm virtually that of the funeral march. The last sound is a gong-stroke: not soft as in previous symphonies, but harsh, imperious, drowning out the other instruments, ringing down the curtain on total darkness and an empty stage. Even after the affirmative finale, the tragedy and mystery remain an ever-present reality.

No sooner had Brian completed Symphony No. 12 in February 1957, than he proceeded from the general idea of Tragedy to the particular play – he set *Agamemnon* as a one-act opera, his fifth and last, and completed the entire 40-minute score before the end of April. The opera is very different from the symphony – an urgent, fast-moving, brutally concise demonstration of Fate in action, where characters are totally subordinated to the onward rush of events. It was the last work Brian wrote at his home in North Harrow, where he had been living since the outbreak of World War II. Two years were to pass before he began to compose again, and in the meantime he moved to Shoreham-by-Sea, on the Sussex coast. There he spent the rest of his life, and there he wrote the series of 20 further symphonies which it will be my task to describe in my second volume.

APPENDIX I

Havergal Brian's principal works up to 1957

(Completion dates generally refer to full scores. The dates of some early works are open to verification. In addition to those works listed as missing, some choral works are known only in vocal score.)

1896   *Requiem* (LOST)
1900   *Tragic Prelude* (LOST)
        Burlesque Variations and Overture (LOST)
1901   *Psalm XXIII*, for tenor, chorus and orchestra
1902   Overture *For Valour*
1903   *By the Waters of Babylon*, for baritone, chorus & orchestra
1904   Symphonic Poem *Hero and Leander* (LOST)
        English Suite No. 1
1906   *Carmilhan*, for soli, chorus & orchestra (LOST)
1907   *Fantastic Variations, Festal Dance* (*A Fantastic Symphony*)
1908   Cantata *The Vision of Cleopatra*
1912   Comedy Overture *Doctor Merryheart*
        Symphonic Poem *In Memoriam*
1913   *Kevlaar*, for chorus & orchestra (LOST)
1914   English Suite No. 2 (LOST)
1918   Burlesque Opera *The Tigers*
1919   English Suite No. 3
1920   Three Preludes for small orchestra (LOST)
1921   English Suite No. 4
1927   Symphony No. 1 in D minor, *The Gothic*
1931   Symphony No. 2 in E minor
1932   Symphony No. 3 in C sharp minor
1933   Symphony No. 4, *Das Siegeslied*
1934   Violin Concerto No. 1 (LOST)
1935   Violin Concerto No. 2
1937   Symphony No. 5, *Wine of Summer*
1944   Cantata *Prometheus Unbound*
1948   *Sinfonia Tragica* (Symphony No. 6)
        Comedy Overture *The Tinker's Wedding*
        Symphony No. 7 in C major
1949   Symphony No. 8 in B flat minor
1951   Opera *Turandot, Prinzessin von China*
        Symphony No. 9 in A minor
1952   Opera *The Cenci*
1953   English Suite No. 5 (*Rustic Scenes*)
1954   Symphony No. 10 in C minor
        Symphony No. 11
        Symphonic Poem *Elegy* (*A Song of Sorrow*)
1956   Opera *Faust*
1957   Symphony No. 12
        Opera *Agamemnon*

APPENDIX II

Manuscripts and Editions

SYMPHONY No. 1, *The Gothic*. The autograph full score of Part I is in the possession of Dr. Robert Simpson. The whereabouts of the full score of Part II are unknown; Cranz & Co. possess an autograph short score which presumably represents the final sketch of the *Te Deum*. A 2-volume full score was published by Cranz in 1932.

SYMPHONY No. 2. The autograph full score is in the BBC Music Library. Autograph sketches are in the possession of the composer's family. A facsimile edition full score was published by Musica Viva in 1973.

SYMPHONY No. 3. The autograph full score is in the BBC Music Library. Autograph sketches are in the possession of the composer's family. Unpublished.

SYMPHONY No 4, *Das Siegeslied*. The autograph full score is in the BBC Music Library. An autograph vocal score, presumably a final sketch, is in the British Museum. Unpublished.

SYMPHONY No. 5, *Wine of Summer*. The autograph full score is in the BBC Music Library. An autograph vocal score, presumably a final sketch, is in the British Museum; an earlier set of sketches is in the possession of the composer's family. Unpublished.

SYMPHONY No. 6, *Sinfonia Tragica*. There are two autograph full scores, exhibiting minor differences in detail. The earlier is in the British Museum; the later (the one used in performance) is in the BBC Music Library. There is also a set of sketches, in the possession of the composer's family. A study score will be published by Musica Viva in 1974.

SYMPHONY No. 7. There are two autograph full scores, one in the BBC Music Library. The other autograph, and a set of sketches, are in the British Museum. A study score will be published by Musica Viva in 1974.

SYMPHONY No. 8. There are two autograph full scores: one in the British Museum, the other in the possession of Dr. Robert Simpson. In addition there exists a complete set of parts in the composer's hand (BBC Music Library) and preliminary and final sets of sketches (in the possession of the composer's family). A facsimile study-score, edited from these sources, was published by Musica Viva in 1973.

SYMPHONY No. 9. The autograph full score is in the British Museum. Autograph sketches are in the possession of the composer's family. A study score will be published by Musica Viva in 1974.

SYMPHONY No. 10. The autograph full score is in the British Museum. Autograph sketches are in the possession of the composer's family. A facsimile study-score was published by Musica Viva in 1973.

SYMPHONY No. 11. The autograph full score is in the British Museum. Preliminary and final sets of sketches are in the possession of the composer's family. Unpublished.

SYMPHONY No. 12. The autograph full score is in the British Museum. Autograph sketches are in the possession of the composer's family. Unpublished.

[Just before publication, all manuscript scores held by the BBC Music Library were returned to the composer's family.]

APPENDIX III

Performances and Recordings

SYMPHONY No. 1, *The Gothic*. First performed at Central Hall, Westminster, on 24 June 1961, by Noelle Barker (soprano), Jean Evans (contralto), Kenneth Bowen (tenor), John Shirley-Quirk (bass), the London Philharmonic Choir, Kingsway Choral Society, London Orpheus Choir, Hendon Grammar School Choir, the Royal Military School of Music and the Polyphonia Symphony Orchestra conducted by Bryan Fairfax. First professional performance at the Royal Albert Hall on 30 October 1966, by Honor Sheppard (soprano), Shirley Minty (contralto), Ronald Dowd (tenor), Roger Stalman (bass), the BBC Chorus, BBC Choral Society, City of London Choir, Hampstead Choral Society, Emmanuel School Choir, Orpington Junior Singers and the BBC Symphony Orchestra conducted by Sir Adrian Boult. A pirated recording of this performance was issued in Los Angeles (Aries LP-2601, 2-record set).

SYMPHONY No. 2. First performed in the Dome, Brighton, on 19 May 1973, by the Kensington Symphony Orchestra conducted by Leslie Head.

SYMPHONY No. 3. A BBC performance, conducted by Stanley Pope, with Ronald Stevenson and David Wilde as pianists, will be broadcast in 1974.

SYMPHONY No. 4, *Das Siegeslied*. First performed in a BBC broadcast of 3 July 1967, by Honor Sheppard (soprano), the Halifax Choral Society, Leeds Philharmonic Choir, and the BBC Northern Symphony Orchestra conducted by Maurice Handford.

SYMPHONY No. 5, *Wine of Summer*. First performed in Kensington Town Hall on 11 December 1969, by Brian Rayner Cook (baritone) and the Kensington Symphony Orchestra conducted by Leslie Head.

SYMPHONY No. 6, *Sinfonia Tragica*. First performed in a BBC broadcast of 21 September 1966, by the Orchestra of the Royal Opera House, Covent Garden, conducted by Douglas Robinson. A performance by the London Philharmonic Orchestra, conducted by Myer Fredman, has been recorded by Lyrita records for release in 1974.

SYMPHONY No. 7. First performed in a BBC broadcast of 13 March 1968, by the Royal Philharmonic Orchestra conducted by Harry Newstone.

SYMPHONY No. 8. First performed in a BBC broadcast of 1 February 1954, by the London Philharmonic Orchestra conducted by Sir Adrian Boult.

SYMPHONY No. 9. First performed in a BBC broadcast of 22 March 1958, by the BBC Symphony Orchestra conducted by Norman del Mar.

SYMPHONY No. 10. First performed in a BBC broadcast of 3 November 1958, by the Philharmonia Orchestra conducted by Stanley Pope. The first recording (Unicorn RHS 313), by the Leicestershire Schools Symphony Orchestra conducted by James Loughran, was released in April 1973.

SYMPHONY No. 11. First performed in a BBC broadcast of 5 November 1959, by the London Symphony Orchestra conducted by Harry Newstone.

SYMPHONY No. 12. First performed in the same broadcast as No. 11. First public performance, at a Promenade Concert, in the Royal Albert Hall, on 4 August 1966, by the BBC Symphony Orchestra conducted by Norman del Mar.

DATE DUE	BORROWER'S NAME	ROOM NUMBER

DATE DUE
